Get A GRIP

Douglas Weiss, PhD

SILOAM
A Strang Company

Most Strang Communications/Charisma House/Siloam/FrontLine/Realms products are available at special quantity discounts for bulk purchase for sales promotions, premiums, fund-raising, and educational needs. For details, write Strang Communications/Charisma House/Siloam/FrontLine/Realms, 600 Rinehart Road, Lake Mary, Florida 32746, or telephone (407) 333-0600.

Get a Grip by Douglas Weiss, PhD
Published by Siloam
A Strang Company
600 Rinehart Road
Lake Mary, Florida 32746
www.siloam.com

Author's Note: The testimonials of individuals in this book are fictitious and created from composites of clients who share similar issues. Names and identifying information have been changed to protect confidentiality. Any similarities between the names and stories of individuals described in this book and individuals known to readers is coincidental and not intentional.

Cover design by Judith McKittrick
Interior design by Terry Clifton

International Standard Book Number: 978-1-59979-152-4

07 08 09 10 11 — 987654321
Printed in the United States of America

Dedication

This book is dedicated to the numerous brave souls who have taken the keys to unlock their chains and have experienced an unprecedented freedom in their lives.

Contents

Table of Charts

Introduction

Welcome to *Get a Grip*! You are in for a totally different ride than what you may have expected within these pages. You are not going to read lengthy pontifications of why you should gain control over what has been controlling your life. You are not even going to see long lists of the types of behaviors you might normally think of as addictive, destructive, or out of control. Instead, you are going to be compassionately but firmly guided along a journey that will show you how to identify behaviors that are in control of your life, and how to fight and win over these areas, even if you have previously struggled with failure and shame. You will be in good hands. I know exactly what it is like to be trapped, addicted, out of control, and unsuccessful in multiple areas of life.

I know what it is like to give your life to God and still experience the feeling of being trapped. Where do you go when you are supposed to be totally free but you still experience failure on a daily basis? That's where *Get a Grip* comes in. You can pick yourself up page by page and do the work that it takes to become free. That's right, I said "work." *Get a Grip* is a practical process that has been proven to work—time after time, day after day, year after year—in my life and in the lives of clients I have served for more than eighteen years in my counseling practice.

I have personally experienced a freedom that I thought I would never have. I remember pleading and begging God, over a period of several years, to help me get and stay free from behaviors that had a grip on me.

Now that I have used the process outlined in this book, I no longer only see the tears of sorrow from those trapped, but now I see the tears of joy from those who have been set free. They are free from that nagging behavior that has controlled them for years. You will meet some of these individuals in these pages, and they will encourage you and help you to not feel alone in your struggle.

Get a Grip is a healing process, not a magic wand. I have met many people who desire a magic potion, a precise prayer, or a person who with one touch of their hand could stop their behavior from ravaging their lives. As Christians we often want the quick and immediate fix to our troubled situation. Unfortunately, God will often allow us to go through a process instead of instantly delivering us from a situation or behavior. Why? I really can't say that I know the exact reason, but I can give you a good guess.

My guess is that God really does love us, and He has an agenda for all of us to look more like Him. If He always instantly did everything for us, we would not develop His character in our hearts and lives.

God ultimately wants our lives to be a reflection of Him. He allows us to stay in our condition until we learn to follow some basic biblical principles that develop His character within us. In my case, I was stuck with an unwanted behavior until I was willing to be transparent about my really yucky condition. When I agreed to follow a process of intense honesty, I became free. I experienced days, weeks, and eventually years of freedom because I was willing to develop the character of honesty. In God's eyes, I believe that developing this character trait was worth the journey that it took for me to get a grip on my out-of-control behavior.

If you look through the Old Testament, you can see God regularly laying out different prescriptions for total victory. *Get a Grip* is the same type of prescription for victory. It is a distinct and proven process that can give you the ability to get a grip on out-of-control behavior in your life. What's even better is that once you apply these strategies to your life, you can actually maintain this victory.

Even more exciting to me and to the many who have applied the *Get a Grip* principles is that they are easily transferable. This means that as you get a grip you can teach as many other people as you want who also desire to get a grip over something that may be controlling them. That means our mess can become our message of hope and healing for others who are struggling. God can use you to help others! He loves using broken vessels that continue to pursue their healing process throughout their life so that they can also give it away to others.

I am excited for you as you pursue your goals. I am very familiar with the journey you are about to take. Like a mountain-climbing guide with a new group of hikers about to embark, I know when the trail will seem too steep to climb, when you will see some amazing sights that will make you *ooh* and *ah*, and I also know how much you will enjoy the entire process.

Everyone has their own journey up the mountain of growth and change. Many of us have obstacles to overcome—otherwise known as behaviors that we just can't seem to get control over. For some of you, the behavior may be rage; for others, it's complacency, apathy, or even addictions to work, food, or exercise.

As human beings we are all so very different. We have all traveled from a different past. Some of us had painful situations that are at the source of our out-of-control behaviors. It is as if we try to climb, but our legs are trapped by roots that need to be untangled before we can even take our first step and begin our uphill climb.

Some have been caught off guard by an avalanche and are buried in the cold snow on the side of the mountain. For these individuals, it takes gathering a rescue team who can dig them out and take them to safety.

There are others who have tried to make the journey without a guide or even a compass. They end up walking in circles. They have walked so hard and long, but they keep coming back to the same place. For them, getting a clear location on what they need to address can be the key.

Regardless of where you are in your journey, you will soon have a way to get a grip and permanently get control over what has been controlling you. In this book you will be given specific strategies that you will put into practice to vanquish the behaviors that have plagued you.

There is work involved. Don't get discouraged, and don't ever get into the habit of telling yourself, "Oh, I have to *do* this or that." No, not at all! Instead, tell yourself, "I *get* to do this in order to be free, to stay free, and to give freedom away to others who are struggling." You are going to be trained not just to *reach* freedom but also to *teach* freedom. Take this course that is before you with joy. It may not necessarily be that you will whistle as you work, but please enjoy the fact that you have been chosen to do the work.

For me, knowing that I was chosen to break down the chains that had kept my family enslaved for many generations was inspirational. At one time in my life, I thought that I had been disqualified by God and that He couldn't possibly use me in any significant way because of all the pain I had been put through during my childhood. Boy, was I wrong!

I had to go through the "get a grip" process. I had to look at some ugly stuff and do some work. But looking back now, I can honestly say that it was worth going through that season of my life. Today, as the author of almost twenty books and having had an international television show, two made-for-television movies about my practice, and many media appearances, I know that God can still use me in unimaginable ways. I also have enjoyed a wonderfully intimate marriage to a great woman for more than twenty years. I have great friends and co-laborers at my office, and life is good.

"Get a grip!" is an expression we use to tell a person to deal with something. That's what this book is about, but it's also about grabbing hold of a new life of amazing potential. I know some of you will turn the pages slower than others. Camp where you need to in order to obtain your freedom; you deserve a free life!

You are to be congratulated! Not because of where you are trapped right now, but for how you can get a grip and then extend your hand and get a grip on others to help them regain control over what is controlling them, too.

Happy traveling.

—Douglas Weiss, PhD

PART 1

Identifying Out-of-Control Behavior

Get A
GRIP

Chapter One

What Is Controlling You?

Barbara was sitting at her desk as Amy—a twenty-eight-year-old who obviously exercised, with great hair and a face to match—walked past. Barb, thirty-five and out of shape, sighed and grimaced as she seethed with envy.

Barb was jealous of Amy, and everyone in the office knew it. The thirty-five-year-old could not seem to find a kind word to say about her hard-working teammate. Oh, by the way, Barb and Amy worked together in the office of the largest church in town.

Barb, like so many of us, truly struggled with envy toward those who had more discipline in their lives. This envy was not limited to Amy. Barb really did not like anyone skinnier or anyone who she believed was more attractive than she was. Barb's negativity toward herself and others was not very appealing, which explained why her three cats were among her closest friends.

This description of Barb paints a picture of what her life was like when she first came to see me. She did not realize that she was being controlled by a vicious cycle of envy and slothfulness—hating people with more self-control while at the same time continuing to eat junk food and candy bars instead of healthier food. But her story did not end there. She was able to get a grip on what was controlling her life.

Chad was forty-seven years old and a very successful businessman. To know Chad was to know about his downtown office building, his pizza parlor, and his booming housing development. Chad had truly worked hard. Actually, he had worked *too* hard.

Chad's wife, Carol, told me that Chad had worked seventy hours a week practically since they had been married twenty-one years ago. The last real vacation they had together as a family was six years ago when Chad's brother had gotten married.

Carol felt alone in her marriage and said she felt like a single mom. She was raising three children, and one had just left for college. Over the years, she had been left to handle most of the challenges of parenting on her own. She had driven the kids to soccer practices, dance, cheerleading, and summer camps while Chad had hardly even noticed.

She loved Chad, but it seemed he was never content. Chad blamed the big house, the new cars, and other investments for why he felt driven to work so hard. Yet Chad did not see the holes he had left in the hearts of his family.

"What is controlling Chad?" Carol asked me. Well, after several sessions, Chad was able to see that his identity was wrapped up in this success image. He truly thought that his worth was defined by his financial bottom line.

He had lived out a lie that he had heard his self-made millionaire dad tell him repeatedly: "A man makes money; a real man makes lots of money."

Chad had attached his beliefs to this fatherly misinformation. He had believed that he was not a real man unless he was at least a millionaire. But there was hope for Chad. He was able to see the errors in this misinformation. He was able to get a grip on what was controlling him.

Sarah was thirty-two, 5 feet 11 inches, and absolutely stunning. She had modeled off and on throughout her life. Sarah had a master's degree in communication and marketing, and she worked for a large PR firm. Oddly enough, she was still single.

At her first visit to my office, she went on and on about her work achievements, but when I asked about her romantic life, she became quiet. Then a hopeless expression came over her. "Won't anybody just love me for me?" she asked as she reached for a Kleenex.

In tears, Sarah described her love life over the past several months. She blamed the long list of failed relationships on the type of guys she met, saying, "They only wanted one thing."

Over time, Sarah was able to see that the problem was not completely the fault of the men she was dating, but that she, too, had an issue. She recalled an incident at age seven when a teenage boy who was visiting her neighbor sexually abused her and threatened her if she told anyone. Sarah had a deep, ugly secret inside that she had never shared with anyone.

Sexual abuse affects everybody differently. The way it impacted Sarah was that she was absolutely terrified of intimacy. She believed that nobody could love her. She felt damaged, sick, and unlovable.

At first, she was unable to see how she sabotaged all of her romantic relationships. When a man began to love her and wanted her to give her heart, she couldn't. She equated intimacy with pain and fear. She could attract men, but she couldn't be close to any of them.

As we worked through the process described in this book, Sarah was able to gain control over the fear of intimacy that had controlled her since she was seven. The last e-mail I received from Sarah said that she was engaged and letting her fiancé know her heart.

Brian was a bear of a man—6 feet 3 inches tall and 240 pounds of solid muscle. When he walked through the door he filled up the door frame. Brian had played sports since age five when he was in the peewee league. Over the years, he had become strong and fast. His teammates and coaches knew they could rely on Brian to get the job done.

When Brian came to see me at age forty-one, it had been eight years since his last professional game. Brian appeared to be clinically depressed; he wanted to sleep a lot. He worked for himself but would regularly not start work until 11:00 a.m.

Nothing seemed to make Brian happy. He could smile easily, but there was no joy in his eyes. Brian was OK as long as he did not need to make decisions. He would get confused, overwhelmed, and either make a scene or storm out of the office.

Brian was married to Ellen, a petite but strong woman. She had encouraged him to come in for counseling after his third attempt at becoming violent with her. She had called 911, and Brian had spent the night in jail. Brian was ready now to look at what was controlling him.

After talking to Brian about how he grew up, it was obvious. Brian's dad had been a violent alcoholic and womanizer. Brian could clearly recall his dad beating his mother until she bled. He remembered that even as an early teen he would hide under the bed if his dad was drinking.

He recalled being called stupid and being told he could not do anything right and that he would never amount to anything. Brian hated his dad, and yet, he was now being controlled by the same anger that had controlled his dad.

After Brian applied some of the principles in this book, he was able to let go of the rage. Strangely enough, after Brian completed the counseling for managing his rage, his depression symptoms disappeared.

He started exercising and regained his focus at work. His wife reported that they became closer than ever and that he was no longer violent at home or at the office. He was also making better decisions. Brian was able to gain control over the rage that was controlling him.

David was a thirty-one-year-old executive climber. He had reached a level of corporate success, but he had been at a plateau for the last few years. David was active in the community; he coached his son's baseball team and helped with the children at home. David was also an eighth-grade Sunday school teacher with his wife, Becki.

To outsiders, David and Becki looked like the all-American, middle-class couple. That is what Becki thought as well, until one day when she was shopping online and had a wild thought. You see, Becki had attended a woman's conference and had heard me speak on sexual addictions. I had explained to the women at the conference how to check the Internet history files and cache if they suspected their husbands of viewing pornography or participating in online relationships. As the memory of the conference flashed through her mind, she thought, *This is silly. David is about as straight as they come.*

Nevertheless, she clicked and continued to click and couldn't believe her eyes. She screamed and cried and then just sat there in her house, feeling alone in her marriage and alone in her life. She thought of calling her pastor or her sister. Alone and sickened, she finally decided to call David at work. "I need you to come home," she said. "I know what you have been doing." And she hung up.

A short time later, David walked through the door looking pale, white, and crazed. "What's going on?" he demanded.

His wife, oddly calm, stated, "I know what you have been doing. I saw it all on the computer. You tell me what's going on."

David defended himself saying that he only met her a couple times and didn't mean for it to go that far.

But as Becki demanded to know the truth, David slowly revealed a sordid story of affairs, prostitutes, and a local adult bookstore. He felt physically sick, crying and screaming that he had tried to stop and that he didn't want to hurt her.

Becki was able to connect to our office the next day. She and David shared the nightmare of David's secret sexual addiction since age fourteen. He revealed a constant diet of pornography, which had only increased when he got the Internet on his computer at work.

Needless to say, David was controlled by lust. As a Christian, he felt he could not tell anyone because people respected him so much.

After counseling and support groups, David found freedom from pornography. He promised Becki that he would take a regular polygraph test to prove to her that his sexual addiction was in remission. As I write this, David has just finished his third year of being squeaky clean.

At their last visit, Becki hugged my neck and even stopped by my wife Lisa's office to thank her for helping to save their marriage. It wasn't easy, but step-by-step David was able to gain control over what was controlling him.

As human beings, we all have our stories to tell. You may identify with Barb's struggle with slothfulness and envy, Chad's identity issues, Sarah's fear of intimacy, Brian's rage, or David's sexual struggles. You, of course, may not have any of these issues, but you have your own story to tell.

Think back through your life; is there a nagging area that seems to crop up again and again, an area of which you never seem to get control? Really, if we are all honest, our stories probably have more than one area in which we struggle.

You may identify more with Tammy. She didn't have a sex, anger, or envy problem. Tammy's problem was quite different. She was a successful Realtor who always dressed impeccably. She drove the current year Mercedes and employed three office assistants. Yet she and her husband, Charles, came in for counseling.

Tammy was an out-of-control spender. It did not matter that she made almost a million dollars in one year. She shopped constantly for the bigger and better. She created lavish vacations and took other families with them, paying all of their expenses as well as her own. If something went wrong in her life or marriage, Tammy left for hours to go shopping. She drove to the next large city where the good shopping malls were and spent hours buying things. If she had a conflict with the children, she would buy them anything to pacify them.

Although she made good money, she and her husband were on the verge of bankruptcy. Spending controlled Tammy. Now that may not seem so bad to some people, but it was hurting her marriage and her family.

With story after story, people walk into my office. These are good people. They try to be responsible, but they feel that something has control over them.

If you feel something has control over your life, or you know someone else who feels this way, there is hope. You do not have to live your life this way. You really can take back control and live a healthy, happy life. I have seen the principles in the following pages set people free. They have worked not only in the lives of those who have come to me for counseling, but in my own personal life as well.

As a counselor I have seen many people walk through the door discouraged and controlled by something. Those who applied the principles in this book, even though it was hard work, left my office encouraged and in control of whatever was controlling them.

You too can finally gain control over what has been controlling you. Regardless of how long you have lived an out-of-control life, you can take steps to be in control again. At times you will be challenged to do some hard work, but for now all you have to do is turn the page to start the journey of taking control over what has been controlling you.

Chapter Two

How Do I Know?

After reading all the stories in the last chapter, you might be asking yourself, *So how do I know if I have something controlling me?* That's a great question to ask!

As a counselor, this is a question I am faced with regularly. Who among us doesn't have some quirk that we deal with? Most of us have what we might call "issues," but what takes them to the next level? Can the same behavior be OK for one person while another has a need to gain control over it?

To help us answer these questions, let's take a look at Travis and Joan. Travis is an athletic thirty-two-year-old lawyer. He runs three times a week and has good friends and a healthy marriage. Travis, however, drinks a Coke in the morning, another around two o'clock, and a third with dinner. Travis has a high metabolism, and sugar and caffeine have no impact on him that he or anyone else can notice.

Joan is single, thirty-four years old, and not athletic. She, like Travis, also has a Coke in the morning while she is getting dressed. She also has one around ten in the morning, one with lunch, one at three o'clock, and another around dinnertime. Joan, however, is greatly impacted by both sugar and caffeine. While enjoying the buzz of a recent glass of soda, she experiences higher productivity and is more talkative and upbeat. But as the effects wear off, Joan reports feeling sluggish and less productive. She has another Coke to pick her up when she feels this way, and this has now become an out-of-control behavior. For her to go a day without a Coke, she believes, would be hell. Travis can go days at a time without a Coke and experience no consequence or any withdrawal symptoms.

You see, both Travis and Joan have the same behavior (several Cokes a day), but for one it is not even an issue, and for the other it is an out-of-control behavior. I can give you story after story of how one person might not have an issue with sports, exercise, alcohol, prescriptions, or work, but when another person does the same thing, he or she has something controlling them.

Back to your original question: so how can you tell? Although there is not an absolute on all controlling behaviors, I will give you a grid for you to discover if you need to get a grip on any of those mentioned. The first determining factor in that grid is broken promises.

BROKEN PROMISES

Even the smallest child knows what a promise is. You can probably remember an incident in your childhood when you used a "pinky promise." That's when you really, really mean something!

If you've never made a "pinky promise," here's an example: Say you just finished baking a batch of chocolate chip cookies, and you have to leave the kitchen to answer the door. Your five-year-old is sitting about a foot away from the cookies that are cooling down.

As you start to leave, you say, "Don't touch the cookies."

The child says, "I promise."

You give him a doubtful look, and he says, "I pinky promise," as you quickly touch pinkies before answering the door.

When you walk back to your kitchen, your child is still sitting there looking at the same number of cookies as when you left. You see that the "pinky promise" was kept, and all is well between you and your patient child.

When something is controlling you, promises get broken. You make light promises to yourself at first, and then these promises get broken. Then you start getting more serious with your promises. You really mean it this time. You try harder, and maybe even "white knuckle" it for a few days, weeks, or months, and then you break your promise again. The behavior creeps back, and once again it has control of you.

So you back up and not only make a promise to yourself, but now you bring God into the situation. "God, I really promise that I won't do this again. I'm sorry, and I really mean it." So you feel better that you made your promise with God. You get a few steps down the road and *bang!*

You can't believe it, but that behavior showed up again. You make "pinky promises" with God, but you keep breaking them. You begin to get discouraged. Now you are desperate.

So you start making promises to your spouse, friends, parents, children, or even the dog. You feel better by promising. They might even feel a little better, especially if they get the brunt of that which is controlling you.

I remember my stepdad, Bob, who was generally a good-hearted man. He had a serious nicotine addiction. He chain-smoked. I remember many nights would go by with him coughing and spitting up in the bathroom sometimes for over half an hour.

Bob later found out he had throat cancer. He promised himself, my mom, and others he would stop smoking. We all felt better that finally he would stop this behavior that had been controlling him.

We were all disappointed when he chose to keep on smoking. Bob had to have his vocal cords removed. Again he promised us he would stop smoking as he lifted the device to help him talk up to his throat. Again we had felt better, and again he failed. This went on until his death. Bob never took control of nicotine. He died when I was in my early twenties.

One of the indicators that something has control over you is that you have a history of broken promises. Look back over your life when you are considering the behavior that has control of you. Do you have broken promises and pinky promises to yourself, to God, to others? Check the box for "Yes" or "No" in the chart below. If you check any in the "Yes" column, you may need to get a grip on something that has been in control of you.

Table 2-1: History of Broken Promises

Person	*Yes*	*No*
Myself		
God		
Others		

ENTITLEMENT

Although many Americans may not use the word *entitlement* in their vocabularies, our society tends to produce people with a sense of it in their lives. You may be familiar with this attitude of entitlement. It is when a person feels that he or she deserves something. "You owe me" is his or her mantra. Identifying entitlement is a very powerful key to determining if something has been controlling you.

Randall, a successful CEO, was a deacon in his church. He was generous both in time and money toward his church and the community. Randall was fifty-four years old with three daughters.

Randall liked to play golf. Now, I don't mean shooting a few holes here and there a couple of times a month. Randall played golf every Thursday morning and every Saturday from 9:00 a.m. to 1:00 or 2:00 in the afternoon. In addition to this, he would regularly take off of work and hit the range, eat at the club, and come home at 8:00 p.m. just in time to put his children to bed or help out a little before he went to bed. This went on throughout his entire adult life.

On the surface, Randall's reasoning sounds rational. "I work hard, make good money, and provide for everybody," he would say. "Why can't I at least play golf?" But in actuality, Randall was *ir*rational about golf. He would become irate if there was any change in his golf routine. He would miss his daughters' dance recitals, cheerleading competitions, and state championship games to play golf. You see, Randall felt *entitled* to play golf—especially on Saturday.

After time in counseling, Randall could see how he made golf a higher priority than his time with his precious wife and daughters and how he bullied them through this felt entitlement.

You see, entitlement is not a *thought* process; entitlement is an *emotional* process in which a person can block out logic or even common sense. Entitlement is a tricky emotion because it often blinds those who feel it.

Most of us have felt entitled to watch our favorite television show, to eat the last doughnut or piece of pizza, to stay longer at the office or gym, or to live with our parents. Oh, and how about all the new toys, gadgets, home repairs, clothes, or other wonderful things we can feel entitled to?

This attitude of entitlement permeates the area of our life that has control over us. Think about conversations or arguments you have had regarding the area that you suspect might be out of control in your life. Is your reasoning for your behavior logical or emotional? If it is emotional, was it based on feelings of entitlement?

This entitlement feeling or attitude doesn't stop with just those around us; it goes a little further. Many people who have something controlling them have a sense of entitlement also toward God. It's as if in their heart of hearts they say to the Almighty, "You can have some parts of my life, but don't You touch that one!"

This entitlement toward God becomes an internal battle for those who are being controlled by something. You see, God is love, and He really does have our best interests at heart. He is saying, "Please give Me this area of your life. It's hurting you and those you love. Please, I want to see you free and capable; give Me this area of your life."

The person who has an out-of-control behavior will often just flat out say "No" to God. This struggle is normal for anyone who is growing spiritually, but as time passes, this entitlement can move into unwillingness, disobedience, and even rebellion against a loving heavenly Father.

If you have an area that you suspect is out of control in your life, examine the feelings of entitlement you have expressed to yourself, significant others in your life, and God. Use the chart below to help determine if your feelings of entitlement are connected to your out-of-control behavior.

Table 2-2: Ways I Have Demonstrated Entitlement		
	Yes	*No*
I have demonstrated entitlement to continue this behavior in my heart.		
I have demonstrated entitlement to others in my life about this behavior.		
I have demonstrated entitlement toward God with this behavior that I am considering.		

LOST OPPORTUNITIES, RELATIONSHIPS, AND FINANCES

One of the telltale signs that a behavior is controlling you is losses—lost opportunities, lost relationships, lost finances, and so forth. Losses come in many forms; some are more obvious, and some can go unnoticed but still be a significant loss.

Lost opportunities

For some, their out-of-control anger, resentment, gossip, lying, inability to be flexible, pornography, or any other behaviors may have cost them a job. I have known several men who flirt, view pornography, are arrogant, lazy, act entitled or ungrateful, and who have lost their job because of it. If the behavior you are questioning has cost you a job, this is an obvious sign that it is a behavior you definitely need to gain control over.

Out-of-control behavior can also cause lost opportunities for people. I have heard someone tell the story of how a CEO of a large company wanted to fill a very lucrative vice president position. He watched the men he was considering for this position in the cafeteria. The one man who was a very strong candidate was walking through the food line. He placed his food and bread on his platter. He grabbed a piece of butter, which cost three cents, and placed it under his bread so the clerk at the checkout couldn't see the butter.

The CEO thought this man was dishonest and willing to take shortcuts. That three cents cost this man many hundreds of thousands of dollars.

Lost opportunities come in many forms, like not going to college, not taking the risk to start a company, not asking to get involved with an opportunity, not investing in real estate or the market, or simply not getting that promotion. If you feel your behavior has cost you some opportunities, it may be controlling you, and you need to get a grip on it.

Lost relationships

Relationships are another key loss due to something that is controlling you. I remember watching a movie about a man who was obsessed with a baseball team. Because of his obsession, he made several mistakes in his relationship with his girlfriend, repeatedly preferring the team to her and almost losing the relationship.

If you have something controlling you, then there are several relationships you may potentially lose. You may lose relationships at work. You may lose relationships with people you have known a long time. You may even damage, distance, or lose family relationships. I have even known men and women who have lost a spouse or two due to out-of-control behavior. The loss of a relationship with your children may also be a result of an out-of-control behavior in your life.

Lost finances

Financial consequences are also a possible reality for those who have an out-of-control behavior. The person whose out-of-control behavior needs attention might spend endless money on clothes, cars, and houses, creating a huge amount of debt. Someone whose out-of-control behavior is procrastination could have their credit impacted, causing financial consequences. Out-of-control behavior that has the consequence of divorce causes a huge financial loss.

Lost ministry opportunities

The loss of ministry opportunities can also be the result of out-of-control behavior. So many people reading these pages are looking for God to use them in some manner. You have had a "spiritual itch" to get involved in some act of serving God. I am not referring to full-time ministry; your desire for ministry involvement may simply mean singing in the choir. But your out-of-control behavior may have prohibited you because of "your reputation." This out-of-control behavior may also have stopped you from seeking out your ministry due to feelings of guilt, shame, or a sense of isolation.

I have seen so many people who, once they were able to get a grip on what was controlling them, felt instantly free to pursue service toward God of one kind or another. Some felt free to be able to lead a small group in their home or to go to the mission field.

Evaluate your life. Do you regret not pursuing service to God in some way? If you have lost ministry opportunities, then this could be a sign of out-of-control behavior.

Review the previously mentioned losses that can occur as a result of out-of-control behavior. Then look on the next page and check off which losses apply in evaluating the behavior you think is controlling you.

Table 2-3: Losses I Have Experienced		
	Yes	*No*
Loss of a job or finance		
Loss of opportunities		
Loss of relationships		
Loss of ministry opportunities		
Other losses		

NEGATIVE CONSEQUENCES

Another way to identify whether you have a behavior that you need to get under control or not is to determine the consequences of your behavior. If a behavior is out of control, then negative consequences are usually in the wake of this behavior. A wake is a path of waves that a boat leaves behind, just a natural outcome of the boat moving through the water. In the same manner, a behavior that is out of control naturally leaves behind a path or trail of negative consequences.

Perhaps Jake's story will help me explain. Jake was a relatively normal twenty-one-year-old single male. He attended college during the day, spent time rock climbing on the weekends, and had a group of good friends he hung around with on a regular basis. But Jake had a behavior that had control of him—driving fast. When he got in his Mustang, he was king of the road. Not surprisingly, the police did not acknowledge his kingship. He received six speeding tickets in one year and faced a court appearance and possible further consequences.

Jake's story is typical of someone who has an out-of-control behavior. He did not expect any negative consequences for his behavior. When he experienced a negative outcome, it did not stop him from repeating the behavior because he still didn't expect anything bad to happen. He found himself in a cycle of repeated behavior and negative consequences.

Paula is just like Jake, except her out-of-control behavior is ice cream. She doesn't like just any ice cream; it has to be Ben and Jerry's. Almost every night before bed she eats a bowl while watching television, and then she goes to bed. The next morning she wakes up and gets on the scale. The weirdest thing happens; she has gained weight again! She is now overweight by forty pounds, and her weight continues to climb.

Albert Einstein has been attributed as having said, "Insanity: doing the same thing over and over again and expecting different results." In the counseling field, we often find this to be true. People repeat the same negative behavior without anticipating that they will experience the same negative results. This is especially true of someone with an out-of-control behavior. They fail to see the "cause and effect" pattern that is taking place right before their very eyes. Instead they continue to repeat the same *cause* while expecting a different *effect*.

Seth was a really sharp young man who had started his own service company. Seth's out-of-control behavior was criticism. His friends didn't come around often because of this behavior. He also lost customers repeatedly because of his critical nature. People like Seth tend to think it is always the other person's fault when they experience negative results in their relationships, even when they encounter similar reactions to their behavior from many different people. Fortunately for Seth, he eventually put two and two together and sought help for his out-of-control criticism. He was able to stop the pattern of lost customers and friendships by changing his behavior.

Negative consequences of out-of-control behaviors come in many forms—legal problems, unmanageable weight, poor health, overwhelming debt, and paralyzing feelings of fear, anxiety, and shame—and many others. If you have a behavior you suspect to be out of control, think about the negative consequences you have experienced as a result. Look for any track record of repeated consequences in your life—similar to the wake from a boat—that just seem to keep going. Take a moment and reflect on this, and then check off below if you believe the behavior you have is controlling you.

Table 2-4: Negative or Repeated Consequences for Out-of-Control Behavior		
	Yes	*No*

FAILED ATTEMPTS TO CHANGE

"It's not my first rodeo!" Jonathan said as he sat in the chair facing me to discuss his out-of-control behavior.

"What do you mean?" I asked with interest.

He went on to tell me about six different attempts he had already made to stop his out-of-control behavior, and how none of them had met with success.

You might be feeling exactly the same as Jonathan; you have tried "this, that, and the other thing" with no success. You read a certain book, went to a specific conference or class, and still have no more success to show for your effort. It seems that the controlling behavior just keeps popping up.

Needless to say, repeated unsuccessful attempts to get a grip on your actions are a very clear sign that the behavior in question has control over you. I personally remember feeling discouraged as I went from one idea to another to get a grip on my out-of-control behavior just to fall back on my face again. I would cry, pray, get up, try the same thing again, and fail. Then after a season of failing, I would give up for a while and just be out of control. *So what?* I would think.

Then I would muster up the strength to either try an old idea again with more conviction, or I would start with a whole new formula for success. Time and effort would pass, and yet again I would ultimately fail.

If you are like me, your struggle to get a grip hasn't just happened over a period of *weeks*. My repeated failures to get a grip on my out-of-control behavior occurred over a period of *years*.

I would get so discouraged that the motivation to try would get less and less. I would at times believe and feel that I could never get free. If you can relate to this experience of repeated failures, you may be controlled by a behavior.

Reflect on this for a moment. Do you have a history of failed attempts to change your behavior? If you can look back and see a pattern of attempts and failures, there is a strong chance you have been controlled by something you need to get a grip on. In the space below, write your response.

Have your repeated attempts to change this behavior met with failure? (Check one.)

- ☐ Yes
- ☐ No

Explain your answer:

____

____

INEFFECTIVE PRAYER

Most of the people reading this book believe in prayer. I really believe in prayer and its power to work in our hearts and lives. James 5:16 says, "Therefore confess your sins to each other and pray for each other so that you may be healed. The prayer of a righteous man is powerful and effective."

I find it interesting that the apostle James connected the concept of confessing sins to the concept of effective prayer in this verse. I believe James wanted us to understand that a person with powerful prayers is a person who stays honest about their faults—a person who is able to recognize their flaws, share them with other people, own them as sin, and move into the healing of these faults. This sincere seeker is the one whose prayer captures God's attention and brings results.

As a counselor for many years, I have found that the reverse of this scripture is just as true—that "he or she who keeps their faults a secret from others doesn't heal, and their prayers don't appear to be that effective."

I have experienced this truth firsthand. I remember when I was in Bible college, I definitely had an out-of-control behavior. I kept this out-of-control behavior a secret from my roommates, my friends, and my pastor. I never even spoke about the subject around others, so asking someone to pray for me was out of the question. During this same time period, I remember it seemed my prayers, although sincere, were going no higher than the ceiling.

I have seen this with many clients as well. As long as they keep their behavior a secret struggle, they stay "sick," so to speak. They remain out of control, and they report praying but with no results.

Now I don't fully understand this, but I have seen this principle work repeatedly in my life and in the lives of others. It might have to do with the fact that God "mocks proud mockers but gives grace to the humble" (Prov. 3:34).

You see, when you are not honest with another person it is usually because of pride. We don't want others to think less of us. We prefer that they think we are more wonderful and less flawed than we actually are in reality.

God likes it when we are open and honest about our flaws. I think part of being humble is being honest about our less-than-wonderful parts. I know it is hard to show this level of humility, but there is something very healthy for the soul when one is being humble. I think God likes a soul that can stay humble.

Take time to think about your prayer life as it relates to the behavior that you are evaluating. Have you prayed and prayed and felt as if you have gotten nowhere? Explain.

____

____

____

____

Do you feel your prayers have been ineffective because of a behavior you suspect is out-of-control in your life?

- ☐ Yes
- ☐ No

Explain your answer:

____

____

____

____

I do want to encourage you that as we open up to others, our prayers can become very effective. I haven't struggled with that out-of-control behavior I had in Bible school for more than eighteen years. I believe God is so much closer to me today and hears my prayers because of my willingness to let go of my secrets.

YOUR HEART

In the King James Version of the Bible, Proverbs 14:10 says, "The heart knoweth his own bitterness; and a stranger doth not intermeddle with his joy." In the New International Version this verse reads, "Each heart knows its own bitterness, and no one else can share its joy."

This scripture and many others like it do not use the word *heart* to refer to a blood-pumping organ that keeps us alive; they use the word *heart* to refer to the seat of our mind, will, and emotions. Our hearts are a very special part of who we are. Our hearts, when we are honest, know the truth about ourselves.

Our hearts know our flaws and weaknesses. Often I ask people to "look into your heart" to see if they know the truth about their situation. Most people do know the truth when they look in their hearts, when they search for the underlying thoughts and emotions that motivate their actions.

When it comes to out-of-control behavior, we often surround ourselves with denial, rationalization, and excuses, but our hearts know the truth. Whether our out-of-control behavior is spending, envy, self-righteousness, controlling, lying, or whatever the behavior, our hearts know the truth.

Being honest with our hearts can take real effort. When I say to my clients, "Now, close your eyes and just go to your own heart. What does it tell you is the truth about this behavior?" it can take several minutes for them to actually hear their hearts.

From the outside it looks as if there is a battle going on inside them. They are often caught up in the lies, reasoning, and justification for their behavior, but their hearts know the truth. Finally, as they push through, they declare the truth that their hearts already knew. "Yes, this is out of control," or "I'm out of control," they'll say.

This heart-level admittance is usually a first step in the beginning of change. An honest heart really does know if you are out of control with some behaviors. I know in our culture we spend so much time in our heads that often our hearts are strangers to us. For some, it could take a little while to locate their hearts. Your heart will tell you the truth; it knows the truth as to whether you are out of control with the behaviors you are considering to be a problem.

Let's stop for a minute. Close your eyes, put the book down, and ask your heart, "Am I out of control with ____________?" Then take a few minutes and really listen to your heart.

TEST YOURSELF

I find it very helpful to my clients when I have them evaluate themselves. It seems to mean more when a person takes a few moments and looks at the big picture before plunging into the solutions. When someone is thoroughly convinced that they have an out-of-control behavior, they are much more likely to stay committed to the process of getting a grip on what has been controlling them.

What about you? The road might get tough, but if you are committed to get to the other side, you go through the bumps to get there. *There*, by the way, is a great place, a life without being controlled by what has been controlling you.

So let's see if you are being controlled by something. List the behavior or behaviors you think might be controlling you. You can do this in the space below or on a separate piece of paper.

Table 2-5: Behaviors That Currently Control Me

Table 2-5: Behaviors That Currently Control Me

Now, let's run them through a self-test to see what you conclude. I have listed below all of the questions I have asked you so far in this chapter. Fill in the top three behaviors you suspect of controlling you across the top of the chart. Then take a moment and answer the questions again, writing "yes" or "no" in each box as it relates to the behavior you've written at the top of each column.

Table 2-6: The GET A GRIP Self Test

	Behavior #1 ____________ ____________	*Behavior #2* ____________ ____________	*Behavior #3* ____________ ____________
Have I promised myself to stop this behavior, and then broken my promise?			
Have I promised others to stop this behavior, and have I broken my promise?			
Have I promised God to stop this behavior, and have I broken my promise?			

Table 2-6: The GET A GRIP Self Test

	Behavior #1 ______ ______	*Behavior #2* ______ ______	*Behavior #3* ______ ______
Have I had entitlement in my heart to continue this behavior?			
Have I demonstrated entitlement toward God about this behavior?			
Have I suffered the loss of a job due to this behavior?			
Have I had lost opportunities due to my behavior?			
Have I suffered losses in relationships due to this behavior?			
Have I lost ministry opportunities due to my behavior?			
Have I had consequences or repeated consequences due to this behavior?			
Have I had repeated attempts at stopping this behavior that have met with eventual failure?			

Table 2-6: The GET A GRIP Self Test			
	Behavior #1 __________ __________	***Behavior #2*** __________ __________	***Behavior #3*** __________ __________
Do I feel my prayers have been ineffective in the past due to this behavior?			
In my heart do I know I am out of control in this behavior?			

As you look over the chart, count how many "yes" answers you have. If you have more than seven "yes" answers in a particular column, the behavior is controlling you. Knowing this information is paramount to getting better. After all, you cannot find a solution for something if you aren't even aware of the problem.

Now, you may have more than three behaviors to work on; however, I would caution you not to try to get a grip on too many behaviors at once. Three is the maximum that most people can handle at one time, which is why I provided three columns in the previous self-test. Most people find it works best to attack one behavior at a time.

Now that I've helped you identify the symptoms of your out-of-control behavior, it's time to learn to recognize the cycle this behavior creates in your life.

Chapter Three

Recognizing the Cycle of Out-of-Control Behavior

In Colorado Springs, we see the Rocky Mountains every day. Aesthetically speaking, these majestic mountains, which include the 14,000-foot-high Pike's Peak, are beautiful. But they also serve a very pragmatic purpose. The Rockies are located on the west side of town. When I am driving I can always gauge if I am going in the correct direction by locating the mountains in the west.

In life, it is also helpful to have identifiable signs to assess the direction in which we are going. When it comes to behavior, it is also good to have a guideline to see if you are headed toward becoming out of control. It is this guideline that I have labeled the cycle of out-of-control behavior. Recognizing this cycle can be helpful if you are trying to identify where you are in an out-of-control area of your life. It's amazing how we can be motivated in one area, sad in another, defensive about a third, and so on.

So, let's take a look at the six stages of the cycle of out-of-control behavior.

THE SIX-STAGE CYCLE OF BEING OUT OF CONTROL

Stage 1—Hopelessness

When you begin to feel hopeless in an area of your life, it might be more than just an emotion. Hopelessness is often the first stage of a cycle that negative behavior produces.

I know this from personal experience. Like so many others who struggle with those extra ten pounds, I have tried everything. I eat less, I eat healthier foods, and I eat early in the day. I exercise regularly, irregularly, do aerobic weights, swim, and bike. Still, there it is staring me in the face—that extra weight I affectionately call "the flub." I feel hopeless about the flub.

Many of us have some flub in our lives. For some of us, the flub can be feelings inside such as hatred, arrogance, or intolerance of others. For others the flub is external, so it is obvious or easy to spot—food, alcohol, sex, work, or entertainment. I knew a man who was controlled by sports. Something had to be very important for him to miss ESPN.

Stage 2—Denial

Because you feel hopeless, you quickly move into stage two of the cycle: you deny that there is any flub. That's easy in my case. I'll binge and then not weigh myself. You see, as long as there is no measure, truth, or fact, I can live very comfortably with my flub. Actually, I can even deceive myself that the flub is getting better when I don't measure the flub.

Denial is the second stage of out-of-control behavior. I know it sounds silly, but denial is one of the easiest ways to tell if someone needs to get a grip on their behavior. Nobody wants to admit that they are out of control, and so we just don't believe it.

I'll never forget a lady who was very overweight and continuing to grow. In public she would eat salads and small portions, but at home she ate chips, cookies, cakes, candy, and ice cream constantly. Her son caught her eating ice cream right out of the container from the freezer.

The son stood there for several minutes just watching this out-of-control behavior. She came up with a story about not wanting to wash the bowl. This confused the son even more since she wasn't the one who did the dishes.

She couldn't just say to her son, "I'm out of control. I just have got to have my ice cream (sugar and carbohydrate) fix before I go back to bed." Instead she denied that her behavior was out of control.

Stage 3—Defensiveness

When someone addresses our flub—the area that is out of control in our lives—we become defensive about the behavior. If they continue to press us on the matter, often we use our emotions to defend our behavior.

Has this ever happened to you: someone suggests to you that you are less than perfect or less than wonderful in an area of your life, and your reaction is defensiveness at the messenger of the truth? That's why prophets in the Old Testament had a tough job. They were responsible to tell the king God's message of truth, and if the king didn't like it, he had the authority to have them killed.

So it is with us. You are out of control with jealousy, and your best friend in the world smilingly states, "It sounds like you could be jealous of them." Then *whamo!* It digs into the core of your being.

You think, *Off with their head!*

Now, if you are married, you might have these types of conversations daily! Spouses have a way of pointing out our flub—sometimes gently and sometimes not so gently. But a defensive response to even the gentlest "reality check" is further proof that you are in a cycle of out-of-control behavior.

Stage 4—Rationalization

Now, we are all intelligent adults, right? I hope so, because this leads us to the next stage of the cycle of out-of-control behavior. After you get over your defensiveness, you will probably move into the stage of rationalization.

You are probably familiar with rationalizing. I don't think I have ever met an adult who does not know how to rationalize. That's when you make up reasons for why you do the things you do: "Everyone does it." "It's not a problem." "I can stop anytime." "I only do it when I am tired." "It helps me relax." "I've worked hard, so I'm entitled to it." "My whole family does it." "I can afford it." "At least I don't…"

There are hundreds of rationalizations for your flub. Suppose your area is pride. Someone points it out, and you just think they're jealous. You rationalize the other person's perceptions so you don't have to look at the pride that others see in you.

Stage 5—Sadness

Rationalizing your flub, or out-of-control behavior, is not the last stage of identifying out-of-control behavior. The next stage of identifying out-of-control behavior is sadness. When I feel like I cannot beat the flub, I get down about it. You can think of areas of your life that you tried to stop being that way, but here you go again.

I knew a man who struggled with being rude. He grew up thinking being rude was funny, and he was not corrected for it. For years he had alienated people from his life, including his adult children. When he came in, he was truly sad about how rude he was to people, sad not just because of how he hurt those he loved, but also sad because he couldn't seem to stop being rude; even when he tried, he failed.

Many have had moments of sadness about an out-of-control area. Sometimes this sadness occurs once and is felt very deeply. My experience is that for many people, this sadness occurs again and again. Sometimes this sadness moves a person to the last stage of the cycle, but often times, people just remain "stuck" in deep sadness for years.

People stuck in sadness wish they could be different, but somehow they just can't "get there." Even if they do seemingly get a grip on what's been controlling them, they cannot maintain long-term victory in their out-of-control area, so the sadness returns.

Stage 6—Motivation

The last stage of the cycle of out-of-control behavior is motivation—you know, that feeling you get when you are ready to fight again, ready to try the new diet, revelation, or program that might work this time. When you are in motivation mode you fully accept your flub. That is to say, you fully accept that you have an out-of-control area of your life.

In the motivation stage you're not hopeless, denying, defensive, rationalizing, or even sad. You are upbeat about your newest attempt to get a grip on life. You are armed with new strategies or information, and you are going to nail this area of your life for good.

What I like about this stage is the honesty. You can clearly articulate, "I'm overweight, lazy, envious, greedy, rude, addicted, or proud." After all, in your mind, this area is dead. It might as well leave now because you are on a crusade to kill this varmint! Well, at least that's the way you feel. Now, if you successfully defeat your enemy you feel great, especially if it stays dead for years and years.

Unfortunately, many of us are just in another chapter in the saga of being defeated once more by this area that is out of control in our life. If you have been through this cycle, you know exactly where this failure takes you: back to—yes, right back where we started—hopelessness. Let's look at this cycle. I find that if my clients can see a picture they can better connect what I am trying to explain. So on the next page is a picture of the cycle of out-of-control behavior.

Seeing the cycle can stir up feelings for people who are stuck in it. If you feel like the stages of this cycle are all too familiar, you can probably relate to the story of the man who walked down the street and fell into a hole. The next day he walked down the same street and fell into the same hole. Sound a little bit like the life you've been living? Don't despair. Read on.

The man went on falling into the same hole for days *until he finally learned to walk on the other side of the street.* You see, there is hope. You don't have to go back to that grim hole of failure again. You can learn to walk on the other side of the street. You can get a grip on the behaviors that control you.

Table 3-1: The Cycle of Out-of-Control Behavior

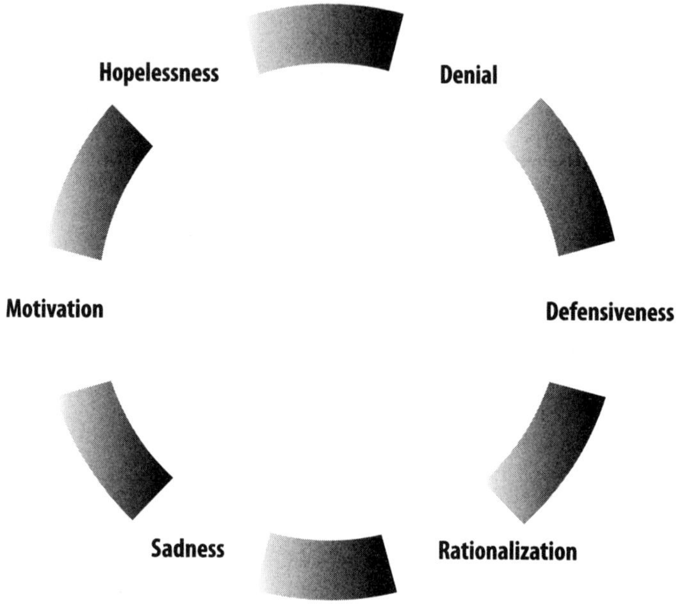

I want you to know that I am not going to leave you stuck in the quicksand of this cycle. In the following chapters I will throw a rope to pull you out of the cycle and give you the skills to not go back into this spot again.

Think back to the behaviors you identified in the last chapter. Now, let's go through each stage of the cycle. Answer the questions carefully. Your answers should reveal which stage of the cycle you are in for each out-of-control area.

STAGES OF THE CYCLE OF OUT-OF-CONTROL BEHAVIOR I HAVE EXPERIENCED

Stage 1—Hopelessness

What behaviors or areas of your life have you felt hopeless to control or change? These types of behaviors are usually conducted when you are alone. So think about a behavior that you do when no one is around. Have you ever wanted to stop, but you just said to yourself, "I can't do it"? Write down in the space below these behaviors and the most recent time when you felt hopeless about each one.

1. Behavior: ______________________________

Describe a time when you felt hopeless to change this behavior.

____

____

2. Behavior: ______________________________

Describe a time when you felt hopeless to change this behavior.

____

____

3. Behavior: ______________________________

Describe a time when you felt hopeless to change this behavior.

____

____

Stage 2—Denial

Now, denial of your out-of-control areas may be a little harder to look at. Try to think of examples where you have been in denial about the behaviors you listed above. Write down the most recent time you found yourself in denial about each behavior.

1. Behavior: ______________________________

Describe a time when you denied the need to change this behavior.

____

____

2. Behavior: ______________________________

Describe a time when you denied the need to change this behavior.

____

____

3. Behavior: ___________________________________

Describe a time when you denied the need to change this behavior.

____

____

Stage 3—Defensiveness

Defensiveness is easier to detect in the cycle of out-of-control behavior because it is usually expressed through an emotional outburst. See if you can recall examples of defensiveness in the areas of your life that have been out of control. Write down the most recent time you experienced defensiveness over each behavior that is out of control.

1. Behavior: ___________________________________

Describe a time when you became defensive regarding this behavior.

____

____

2. Behavior: ___________________________________

Describe a time when you became defensive regarding this behavior.

____

____

3. Behavior: ______________________________

Describe a time when you became defensive regarding this behavior.

____

____

Stage 4—Rationalization

Rationalizations tend to come in multiples. For example, if the behavior you list is “Spending,” the rationalizations might be: “I work hard, so I should do as I please.” “It’s not as bad as other people’s problems.” “I haven’t gone bankrupt, so there’s no problem.” In the space below list your behavior and then examples of your most recent rationalizations for continuing this behavior. Include your best guess for the most recent date when you used each rationalization.

1. Behavior: ______________________________

Rationalizations for this behavior:

1. ______________________________
2. ______________________________
3. ______________________________
4. ______________________________
5 ______________________________
6. ______________________________
7. ______________________________
8. ______________________________
9. ______________________________
10. ______________________________

2. Behavior: ______________________________

Rationalizations for this behavior:

1. ______________________________
2. ______________________________
3. ______________________________
4. ______________________________
5 ______________________________
6. ______________________________
7. ______________________________
8. ______________________________
9. ______________________________
10. ______________________________

3. Behavior: ______________________________

Rationalizations for this behavior:

1. ______________________________
2. ______________________________
3. ______________________________
4. ______________________________
5 ______________________________
6. ______________________________
7. ______________________________
8. ______________________________

9. ____

10. ____

Stage 5—Sadness

The sad moments are sometimes very quiet moments for the soul. These are times when you hit a low about the out-of-control areas of your life. In the space below write examples of your sad moments connected to the behaviors in question, along with the time you most recently felt this way.

1. Behavior: ____________________________________

Describe a time when you felt saddened by this behavior.

____

____

2. Behavior: ____________________________________

Describe a time when you felt saddened by this behavior.

____

____

3. Behavior: ____________________________________

Describe a time when you felt saddened by this behavior.

____

____

Stage 6—Motivation

As we have had cycles of the out-of-control behavior, we also have had experiences of motivation. Below record your most recent time of feeling motivated to change each behavior.

1. Behavior: ____________________________________

Describe a time when you felt motivated to change this particular behavior.

____

____

2. Behavior: ______________________________

Describe a time when you felt motivated to change this particular behavior.

____

____

3. Behavior: ______________________________

Describe a time when you felt motivated to change this particular behavior.

____

____

Recognizing where you are in the cycle of out-of-control behavior is the final step in your evaluation of the problem in your life. What we have been doing in part one of this book is similar to what happens when we visit a doctor's office. His first step is evaluation and diagnosis of our condition. As patients we are usually aware of the symptoms of our condition, but it is amazing that after some experienced questioning from a doctor, an accurate assessment of the condition causing those symptoms is reached.

The same is true for our journey through *Get a Grip.* Now that I have led you through some questions and self-analysis tools born from my experience as a counselor, we are at the tail end of identifying or "diagnosing" what has been out of control in your life. Before you picked up this book, you were probably aware of the *symptoms* of the problem—the behaviors or consequences you have been experiencing—but hopefully as you read on, you will become aware of the cause of those symptoms or behaviors. Don't be discouraged; be encouraged. Identifying the real problem leads to the solution. Read on as we continue our journey.

PART 2

Origins of Out-of-Control Behavior

Get A GRIP

Chapter Four

Where It All Started

C. S. Lewis once said, "With the possible exception of the equator, everything begins somewhere." Everything has a beginning. It's true—no matter where you are right now, you have come from somewhere.

All of us spent time in the womb. Although none of us remember any of that warm, bouncing time with Mom, we all still know we started there. That is how it is with our out-of-control behaviors; each one definitely had a beginning. Similar to being born, which most of us do not remember, we may be less than aware of how our out-of-control behavior began.

Just as we all come from different countries, states, cities, and streets, so does our out-of-control behavior. For some of us our out-of-control behavior started in country A in city B. For others with the exact same out-of-control behavior, it started in country C in city D. Allow me to explain.

Lanna was a thirty-four-year-old married woman with four children. Lanna's out-of-control behavior was twisting reality to the point that she would be lying. As she went through the process of getting a grip, which I will outline for you in chapters six through thirteen of this book, she became honest about a sexual abuse incident she was twisting around in her mind as being her fault. This incident of sexual abuse was the genesis, the beginning, of her choosing to lie and make things to be different than they really were.

Derek, a 6-foot 4-inch man who looked like a football player, also had a difficult time with lying. Derek was always sharply dressed, as were his wife and children. Derek had the appearance of being successful, but behind the scenes were huge amounts of credit card debt and personal loans from family and church members that amounted to over $100,000.

Derek wasn't sexually abused. Derek came from a single-parent home and had been abandoned by his dad. His mother was consistently shopping and getting herself fixed up for her new "friends." Derek was always dressed well for school and church. "You need to look good to be accepted and loved" was the message that his mother modeled to him. Derek's major influence to choose to lie was modeled by his mother and some desire to be loved through appearance.

Both Lanna and Derek had a problem with lying, but the origin of the influence to lie was from a different "city," so to speak. In the next several pages, we are going to travel to several different "cities" from which the influence of out-of-control behavior can originate. I call them "cities of origin."

You will probably not have experienced every city of origin in your life. You will probably be tempted to skip a city here or there, but I would encourage you not to. "Why?" you ask. You will meet many people throughout your life who have something that is controlling them. The influence of the behavior that is controlling them may come from a different city of origin than yours. If you read about it while you are trying to get a grip on what is controlling you, you in turn may find out what is controlling them, and you may be able to help them, too.

ABANDONMENT

The city of abandonment is often a cold and windy city. Abandonment comes in many different forms. I will do my best to visit several of the neighborhoods of abandonment.

Total abandonment

The downtown of abandonment is called total abandonment. Total abandonment is the abandonment of a parent—whether intentional or unintentional. The intentional abandonment could have happened if you were born as the result of an unplanned pregnancy and one or both of your parents decided not to be a part of your life. If your parents sent you to live in foster homes, live with relatives, or sent you to boarding schools, you have definitely visited the downtown of total abandonment.

These types of abandonment are intentional by one or both of your parents. In some cases, their intentions were totally selfish. They didn't want you. They wanted to live their own lives, to chase their dreams, lovers, or careers. Some parents' motives are less selfish; they may have wanted to give you a chance at a better life.

Sometimes total abandonment is completely unintentional: one or both parents may become physically or mentally unable to care for a child, or they may die. Whether intentional or not, the downtown of total abandonment may be the origin of the behavior that has control over you.

The neighborhoods around downtown break up into several suburbs. Each suburb represents a part of you that was abandoned or neglected by one or both parents. We will make short trips into these neighborhoods since you may have been to one of them before.

Spiritual abandonment

The abandonment of your spirit is our first suburb to visit in the town of abandonment. In this part of town there are no churches or spiritual influences of any kind. The air is hot and the ground is dry. There is no wind blowing and no water supply.

If one or both of your parents have abandoned you spiritually, you would not have received any spiritual training or encouragement to develop the spiritual aspects of yourself as a child. Spiritual abandonment feels as if your parents decided that you did not have a spirit, so they spent very little or no time communicating spiritual matters. Your contact with a community of faith would have been totally absent.

Another form of spiritual abandonment would have been if one or both of your parents were so rigidly religious you weren't allowed to explore honest questions of a spiritual nature. You were expected to adhere to their belief system without any guidance or encouragement along the way.

Emotional abandonment

The next abandonment you may have experienced is abandonment of your emotions. Emotional abandonment is a confusing area of town. It is as if the city engineers forgot to put names on the streets. You travel down an unknown street to get to another street that you do not know.

In the United States, incidence of one or both parents emotionally abandoning their children is commonplace. It was probably unintentional—I don't think Mom and Dad had a business meeting and said, "Hey, let's abandon our children's feelings." Remember, it is more than likely that your parents' feelings were abandoned as well. They were probably raised by parents who adhered to the old-fashioned and unhealthy mind-set that "children are to be seen and not heard," and they may have carried on this unhealthy mind-set when raising you.

In families where emotional abandonment is taking place, several things occur to the emotional part of the children's beings. They learn that feelings are not valid at all; they might be taught that they are not to identify, trust, or feel a feeling. If they are feeling full while eating, they shouldn't listen to their bodies as they communicate a feeling of being satiated; they should still "eat what is on your plate."

An emotionally abandoned child learns that he should not cry if he feels like crying: "Big boys don't cry." He receives so many mixed messages that tell him his emotional self is not vocal, not trustworthy, or not important. He then in turn has very little training on how to identify or communicate his feelings. He also will have little training on how to utilize feelings in a decision-making process. This can lead him to stay totally "in his head" or be so emotionally based in decisions that he keeps making more bad decisions.

A child from the suburb of emotional abandonment will rarely learn what it is like to be emotionally honest and available in an intimate relationship. I think you can see how visiting the suburb of emotional abandonment as a child can definitely be a genesis for the influence of out-of-control behavior.

Gifting abandonment

Abandonment of your gifting is another stop on this tour. This suburb is confusing as well. It's like you are in a part of town that speaks a different language and has a different currency than you. One or both of your parents have not investigated your particular gifts. They may not have allowed you to experiment with various sports, music, or art to see what your natural aptitude might have been.

Another form of abandonment comes from your parents not allowing you to develop a gift they knew you had. You may have been athletic, musically inclined, just like to fix things, or ask a lot of questions. Your parents wouldn't allow you to develop a gift they actually knew you possessed. This lack of accepting and nurturing your giftedness can definitely be a genesis for an out-of-control behavior.

Affection abandonment

The abandonment of affection is familiar to many trying to get a grip on their life. The climate in this suburb is cold as ice. There is no warmth or shelter from the bone-chilling arctic air.

The abandonment of affection starves the soul of its built-in need (not desire) to be touched, hugged, and have physical affection. All babies are born with this need for affection, and the need continues lifelong. If children are raised in homes where one or both parents fail to nurture this need for affection, they are confused because their bodies really want a hug, cuddle, a pat on the back, or just to wrestle. The abandonment of affection is definitely a place for an influence of behaviors that can get a grip on you.

Financial abandonment

Financial abandonment has two neighborhoods. The rich live on the north side on "Keeping Up With the Joneses Boulevard." The poor, in debt, struggle to make ends meet on the south side at "Buy Now, Pay Later Avenue." The interesting thing about this town is that there are more stores, shopping malls, restaurants, and entertainment outlets than in any other neighborhood in the state. During the day, a never-ending stream of enticing aromas, glittery advertisements, and catchy jingles fill the air. But at night, an army of debt collectors patrol the streets while the repo-man makes his rounds.

These neighborhoods are no place to raise a family, and yet there are many who grow up here. When one or both parents financially abandon their children, they may grow up not understanding finances at all. Nobody teaches them about saving, investing, and how money actually works. Later on, as adults, they may feel inadequate even if they earn well.

Often, parents who financially abandon their children will expose them to either the "work/spend existence" model or the "mystery" model of money. In the "work/spend existence" model, parents live from paycheck to paycheck, never having any money left over to save or invest. In the "mystery" model, parents may be making very wise choices with their money, but they exclude their children from knowing anything about their finances.

Parents who neglect to teach their children the financial aspects of life rarely do this intentionally. I have found that a trail of financial abandonment often goes back for several generations in a family tree. This financial abandonment can most definitely be an influence in controlling behavior.

Sexual abandonment

This suburb is rampant with billboards that encourage the exchange of sexuality for love, acceptance, or pleasure. Sultry and seductive opportunities present themselves on every street corner, waiting to lure their next victim into the tangled vines of pregnancy, disease, and shame. Strengthened by their deep roots, these vines twist and turn along the ground, ensnaring their prey and choking the life out of them.

Sexual abandonment, which is very common in our culture, also tends to run far back in the family tree. Parents in these families raise their children as if they are really not sexual. They send either no message at all, or they send confusing mixed messages such as, "Sex is bad and nasty, and you should save it for the one you love," as one client told me her parents insinuated.

Being sexual is part of being created in God's image. Both Adam and Eve were sexual beings before they ever engaged in any sexual behavior. Being sexual is part of who we are, and it will be for as long as we are living and breathing.

Managing sexuality without clarity from one's parents is difficult. The suburb of sexual abandonment is a common breeding ground for addictive behaviors that control our lives, and the roots of behavior from this neighborhood can be some of the strongest roots of all.

Moral abandonment

The suburb of moral abandonment is a smoggy neighborhood. Things are not very clear here, but it isn't anyone's fault. There's no right or wrong, and no one is responsible for anything.

Morality tells people what is absolutely right and absolutely wrong, and it is an essential ingredient for navigating life with as few crashes as possible. Morality has been given a bad rap in a culture that wants us to be led by our feelings so others can manipulate us. Parents can avoid this by being very clear about right and wrong.

But if you've been to the suburb of moral abandonment, you know that some parents fear being misunderstood or judged by others. Some parents are unclear on moralities, even the basics, due to issues in their own lives such as lying, stealing, or monogamy.

Regardless of the reason for moral abandonment, it is a bastion for the influence of what can later get a grip on someone's life.

Now that you have taken the tour, reflect for a moment on your own journey as a child. Did you visit or live in any of the suburbs of abandonment? For some of you, this realization might be a breakthrough to understanding what has led to the behavior you are currently trying to overcome. Below is a list of the areas of abandonment I have already mentioned. You can check off any boxes that you feel apply to you. (If you are thinking about someone else to whom this may apply, you can take a separate sheet of paper and fill it in based upon your limited information of what abandonment experiences they might have had.)

Table 4-1: Areas of Abandonment That Apply to Me

- ☐ Total abandonment
- ☐ Spiritual abandonment
- ☐ Emotional abandonment
- ☐ Gifting abandonment
- ☐ Affection abandonment
- ☐ Financial abandonment
- ☐ Sexual abandonment
- ☐ Moral abandonment

This town of abandonment is a big city with many suburbs. Some of us have lived in just one part of town. Some of us have been moved from one part of town to another part of town during our developing years. Regardless of the neighborhood (or neighborhoods) of abandonment you may have lived in, the following chapters can help you break your ties to them so you can now live where there is acceptance, love, and peace. But before we move on to the next chapter, we need to visit a few more cities that are possible beginnings for those who are struggling with out-of-control behaviors.

ABUSE

The next stop on our tour of cities of origin is the rough-and-tumble town of abuse. In this city of origin, rubble from bombed-out buildings lines the streets. Fires burn in the distance, and the sounds of gunfire and sirens fill the air. Even in broad daylight, an uneasy tension in the atmosphere alerts visitors that it is unsafe.

Abuse is the intentional violation of another person's spirit, soul, or body, including their emotions and sexuality. The experience of abuse damages a person on many levels, and no two people will be affected in exactly the same way. For some people, abuse damages memories and self-esteem and causes posttraumatic stress and addiction. For others, it affects the choices they make and causes all kinds of dysfunction. Abusing a person is similar to taking a Colt 44 and blasting it into a computer. There is no telling exactly *how* it will damage the computer, but you can be certain that it *will* be damaged.

Physical abuse

It is usually easy to know if you have visited the violent neighborhood of physical abuse—physical harm from a parent, sibling, neighbor, schoolmate, or stranger. You know if you have been hit, kicked, shoved, or physically harmed in some way. Sometimes the abusive action is repeated over and over again, resulting in severe injury. Sometimes, as in the case of parental abuse, it can be ongoing for several years. Physical abuse can also include demanded physical tasks that were cruel or far beyond your ability as a child.

Emotional abuse

On the outskirts of town we find the minefield of emotional abuse. In this city of origin, the ground is barren and empty except for the occasional animal carcass or drifting tumbleweed. But don't let the silence fool you; one false step can be deadly.

Emotional abuse is a common precursor among those who are trying to regain control of their lives. Like physical abuse, it is fairly easy to identify past instances of emotional abuse. Children who experienced emotional abuse during their growing-up years had parents or other people of influence who yelled at them or shamed them. As children, they may have been enmeshed as surrogate adults in their families. Often, they were made to feel guilty just for being a child or for being themselves. This chaos and unpredictability can definitely be an influence in one's soul life and can set people up for out-of-control behaviors later in life.

Spiritual abuse

The neighborhood of spiritual abuse, with its barbed-wire fences and blinding searchlights, is a little trickier to recognize than emotional or physical abuse. In this neighborhood there are no explosions or gunshots to detect, but the atmosphere is smothering. Hidden cameras watch your every move, and the homeowner's association has posted its rules and bylaws on every corner.

Spiritual abuse occurs when a significant religious (not necessarily spiritual) person demands total compliance to a religious belief. This person is shaming, controlling, and often so rigid it is difficult to be in relationship with them. The abusive spiritual leader conveys the idea that being right is more important than love. Rules are more important than relationships in a spiritually abusive environment.

The effects of spiritual abuse vary from person to person: some feel confused, some question their own spiritual development, and some forfeit all spirituality for fear of being controlled by others. Spiritual abuse is definitely one experience that predisposes people to future out-of-control behaviors.

Sexual abuse

Unfortunately, far too many people have visited this city of origin. Hidden deep underground, it is a dungeon-like labyrinth full of horrible, torturous experiences. Sexual abuse is one of the most damaging types of abuse that a person can encounter. The sexual shame often attached to this experience—whether one time or multiple experiences—is overwhelming for the child, teen, or adult.

Sexual abuse is often kept secret and often poorly received when finally disclosed. This can lead to more issues for the survivors of sexual abuse to deal with. The repercussions of sexual abuse, especially if that abuse continues to be a secret, are multidirectional, meaning that they affect many different areas of a person's life. This influence is often an anchor for future out-of-control behavior.

Whatever neighborhood of abuse you may have been through, you certainly didn't choose the abuse, nor did you deserve it. Yet you still suffer great consequences as a result of the abuse, and the responsibility for finding a healthy way to deal with what has happened to you lies solely in your court.

I liken this to a person walking downtown on a sunny afternoon. Suddenly a gunshot is heard, and a bullet strikes her. She didn't ask for someone to shoot her. She didn't deserve the bullet; nevertheless, her injuries are now a reality she has to face. The pain management and physical therapy to restore healing to her injured body are now her responsibility.

You see, you can't control everything that happens to you—no one can—but you can control your reactions. You can control the effect that negative experiences have on your life by how you handle them or deal with them. When you take responsibility for finding healthy ways to deal with what has happened, you are beginning to get a grip on those things that have been out of control in your life.

As you journey to uncover the source of your out-of-control behavior, an important step is acknowledging the abuses that have occurred. This sounds simple, but for many, it can be a huge hurdle to overcome.

There are many roadblocks to acknowledging an abuse. Many sexual abuse survivors tend to beat themselves up about what they wish they had done. This deeply rooted self-blame can cause them to deny the abusive events that have occurred. To protect themselves, they create a façade of complete control, and they are not willing to shatter the image they have made of themselves. They may also fear being honest regarding the abuse. I know several clients who felt that if they were honest about their abuse, then they would decompose uncontrollably and never be sane again. It may sound irrational, but when you are afraid, being rational is not a requirement.

Let's pause for a moment to allow you to take this important step toward getting a grip on your life. It's time to put aside the fear and blame that may be causing you to deny what has happened to you. Regardless of how recently or how long ago the experience has taken place, you must acknowledge that it has happened if you are ever going to experience a life that is free from the shame and bondage of the past. Place a check next to the types of abuse you feel you have experienced.

Table 4-2: Areas of Abuse That Apply to Me

- ☐ Physical abuse
- ☐ Emotional abuse
- ☐ Spiritual abuse
- ☐ Sexual abuse

SHAME

The twin cities of shame are our next destination on our quest to find the origins of out-of-control behavior. They are located on two sides of the same river and connected by a large bridge. Many who spend time in the first city unwittingly find themselves visiting the second. You won't see anyone walking around outside in either town. Privacy is of utmost importance here. Shades are perpetually drawn, and doors and windows are locked up tightly. Let's take a closer look at these two cities of origin.

Sexual shame

Many who are trying to get a grip on what is controlling them may be harboring sexual shame. The experience of sexual shame is attached to very specific events, the memories of which can haunt individuals for decades.

Let's face it: many people have done things of a sexual nature that they are not proud of. For some, this shame includes years of viewing pornography and masturbation. For others, it may be premarital sex or a homosexual encounter they never told anyone about. For still others, the shame of an extramarital affair or other sexual behavior plagues their conscience.

Shame from abortion

Shame from an abortion is the king of secrets. For both men and women, aborting a child is probably one of the darkest things in which they have ever participated. Millions of abortions have been carried out in our culture, which means twice as many as this number have participated in them.

The one most obviously impacted by this event is the woman who participated in an abortion. Counseling women for almost two decades, I can tell you that women who have participated in an abortion have huge issues relating to the experience.

The gut-wrenching tears I have watched from women of all ages, races, and religions tell me this pain, shame, fear, and self-loathing are universal. Regardless of the pressure she may have had from others to abort, abortion is a huge area that influences future out-of-control behavior.

Abortion, however, does not just impact the woman; it also impacts the man who participates in the abortion. I have counseled many men over the years who had to work through their issues around the abortion, and it was very deeply emotional and life-changing for them. For the man, the secrecy and shame about participating in an abortion also influenced future out-of-control behavior.

Your secrets, especially sexual secrets, can definitely be a birthing ground for influences for future out-of-control behavior. Don't worry; we won't keep you hanging in the pages to come. You will learn how to walk out of your sexual shame and be fresh and clean all over again.

Sexual shame is often the hardest to overcome. I do not recommend that you write these behaviors in this book. It is important, however, for you to be honest with yourself. On a separate sheet of paper write out in very direct statements the experiences that have caused your sexual shame.

Abortion, similar to sexual shame, is *not* something I would have you record in this book. However, whether you are a man or a woman, this could be a life-changing event with tentacles in the behavior that has control of you. On a separate sheet of paper write down the issues pertaining to the abortion you participated in.

Once you write down these events, you can destroy the paper—burn it, shred it, black it all out, or do whatever you want to destroy it. There is no need to have a permanent record of your sexual shame; however, there is a need for you to be honest with yourself about it.

In the space below, list the day you wrote out the experiences that have caused you to live in shame.

For the Record
I wrote down my shameful events on

______ ______, 20______.
(Month) *(Day)* *(Year)*

MODELING

Now we'll talk about modeling—not the kind of modeling where someone walks down a runway wearing clothes you cannot afford. Rather what I mean by modeling is the behavior, attitudes, and beliefs that your parents or significant people in your life modeled before you.

This final city of origin for out-of-control behavior has a town square filled with larger-than-life statues and sculptures mounted high on pedestals. Sunlight casts a radiant glow upon the towering monuments that appear to turn up their noses at passersby.

All of us know that if you hang around an angry person, you are much more likely to behave angrily. If you hang around a kind person, you will probably become kinder. We as humans tend to imitate the behavior of those around us.

But even though we have this tendency, each one of us has a choice as to whether or not we will duplicate the positive or negative behavior around us. We don't always make this choice on a conscious level, but we do have a choice. Instead of accepting the behavior of those around us as normal, sometimes we need to stop and evaluate a behavior, question the reasons behind it, and decide what to do with it.

Allow me to share this classic preacher's story to illustrate what I mean. It was Christmastime, and a little girl was watching the women of the household prepare the Christmas dinner. As she watched her mother prepare the ham, the little girl noticed that the mother cut off the end of the ham. The little girl curiously asked her mother why she cut off the end of the ham.

The mother stopped, thought for a moment, and then said, "I really don't know. Go ask Grandma. That's how she taught me to prepare a ham." Grandma also thought for a few minutes, and she really didn't know either. Grandma told her to go ask Great-grandma. Great-grandma just smiled and said, "Years ago, our ovens weren't big enough for the whole ham, so when I would make a ham, I would cut the end off to make it fit in the oven." All the women had a laugh about this. The younger ladies had duplicated a behavior without ever knowing why it was done that way. Likewise, many of us have repeated the behavior of friends, co-workers, and especially family without giving much thought as to why we do their behaviors.

I don't know of a family where you don't hear things such as, "You are just like your dad," or "You are a lot like Mom." As children, our parents modeled all kinds of behavior for us. We absorb these behaviors and duplicate them, often without even realizing that we are doing it.

This reminds me of an observation I made when I recently had my father-in-law and mother-in-law at my house. My father-in-law is a godly man who loves to read the newspaper. My wife inherited this trait, and one of my children also has a strong interest in reading the news. It was funny to see all three of them reading the newspaper at once.

So what's my point? The influence of a role model can be the starting point of an out-of-control behavior that has developed in someone's life. This is not to blame a parent, family member, or friend, but rather to locate the origin of a behavior.

If your nightly ritual before bed was to have ice cream, as a child this was probably not a problem because your metabolism just ate up those extra calories. But as you hit thirty, forty, fifty, and sixty, that same ice cream before bedtime can become a problem because now it is stored in your body as fat and can contribute to something that has control of your life.

Now, as an outsider to your family, I have absolutely no idea what behaviors you had an opportunity to duplicate. You are the expert who will have a great handle on the behaviors you saw growing up. Categories are provided below for you to reflect on the behaviors in your family. Either in the space provided or on another sheet of paper, briefly describe some of the behaviors from Mom and Dad that you would have seen modeled in your home. Keep in mind that you are listing their *behaviors*—not what they might have tried to teach you verbally about a topic.

Table 4-3: Behaviors Modeled by My Parents

	Mother	Father
Social		
Friends		
Co-workers		
Extended family		
Neighbors		
Church folk		
Spiritual		
Church attendance		
Scripture reading		
Sunday school		
Small group attendance		

Table 4-3: Behaviors Modeled by My Parents

	Mother	Father
Recreational		
Spontaneous fun		
Planned vacations		
Sports		
Music		
Travel		
Adventures		
Hiking		
Biking		
Hobbies		
Sexual		
Positive conversations		
Negative conversations		
Never talked about it		
Showing affection		
Hugs were common		

Table 4-3: Behaviors Modeled by My Parents

	Mother	Father
Touching each other		
Wrestling		
Cuddle with parents		
Parents cuddled together		
Financial		
Talked about it		
Didn't talk about it		
Taught to invest		
Taught to save		
Taught to tithe		
Fought about		
Handled together		
One person handled		
Emotional		
Talked about feelings		
Didn't talk about feelings		

Table 4-3: Behaviors Modeled by My Parents		
	Mother	Father
Accepted your feelings		
Feelings were brought up later		
Handling conflict		
Conflict was normal		
Avoided conflict		
Dominated others in conflict by anger		
Dominated others in conflict by silence		
Morality		
Absolute right and wrong		
Right and wrong are circumstantial		
No right and wrong		
Follow your own heart or feelings		
Marriage		
Quality time for just Mom and Dad		
Mom and Dad dated regularly		
It's all about the kids		

Table 4-3: Behaviors Modeled by My Parents		
	Mother	Father
Mom and Dad spent some time away without the children		
Read about marriage		
Attended marriage retreats / conferences / seminars		
Marriage talked about positively		
Respecting spouse was more important than being right		
Verbally praising spouse regularly		

These are just a few categories for you to reflect upon the behavior that was modeled for you growing up. Some of these behaviors are now being duplicated either positively or not so positively in your life today, but tracking the origin of these behaviors may help you to get a grip on what is controlling you.

Now I want to go a little further with the topic of modeling. We not only imitate the behavior of others, we can also duplicate their attitudes or beliefs. These attitudes or beliefs can contribute to whatever has control over your life as well. Since your out-of-control behavior can be almost anything, let's walk through some major areas and record what you believe were the attitudes or beliefs from Mom and Dad that you experienced.

Table 4-4: Attitudes and Beliefs Modeled by My Parents

	Mother	Father
Social		
All people are equal.		
Different races are not equal.		
Income determines the value of a person.		
Have friends, but talk about them negatively.		
Gossip is acceptable.		
Co-workers are friends.		
Co-workers are not friends.		
Extended family is important.		
Extended family gets praise; focus on them positively.		
Tolerate or avoid extended family.		
Respect your neighbors.		
Avoid your neighbors.		
Church friends are important.		
Church folks are hypocrites.		

Table 4-4: Attitudes and Beliefs Modeled by My Parents

	Mother	Father
You have to be perfect.		
Others have to be perfect.		
Spiritual		
God is the boss.		
Consult God only if in trouble.		
Church is important.		
Church is not important.		
The Bible is important.		
The Bible is not important.		
Spiritual friends are important.		
Spiritual friends are not important.		
Recreational		
Fun is important.		
Fun is not important.		
Fun is something you plan for.		

Table 4-4: Attitudes and Beliefs Modeled by My Parents

	Mother	Father
Fun is something you have regularly.		
Fun is inexpensive and available.		
Fun is expensive and unavailable.		
Being athletic is fun.		
Experimenting with different interests is fun.		
Music of all kinds is acceptable.		
Spiritual music is fun.		
Traveling is part of fun.		
Adventure was part of the family.		
TV is most of our fun.		
Video games are our fun.		
Fun has to be educational.		
Sexual		
Only Mom can talk about it.		
Only Dad can talk about it.		

Table 4-4: Attitudes and Beliefs Modeled by My Parents		
	Mother	**Father**
Sex was a subject to avoid.		
Sex was dirty, nasty.		
Good folk don't talk about such things.		
God made sex beautiful.		
Somehow the devil and sex go together.		
Sex is perverted.		
Sex and spirituality are separate.		
Don't you talk about it.		
Showing affection		
Bodies need to be touched.		
Affection is good and valued.		
Asking and receiving affection is good.		
We love hugs.		
Kisses were a way to express love or kindness.		
Nobody touches around here.		

Table 4-4: Attitudes and Beliefs Modeled by My Parents

	Mother	Father
Hugs, kisses are not permitted.		
To need to be touched is weak or weird.		
You're needy if you need affection.		
Financial		
Finances are spiritual.		
Saving was taught as part of life.		
Spending was out of control.		
Go in debt for everything.		
Own real estate.		
Invest in the market.		
Plan for retirement.		
Plan college funds.		
Money is about right now.		
Money is only about the future.		
Money is both now and the future.		

Table 4-4: Attitudes and Beliefs Modeled by My Parents

	Mother	Father
Tithing is critical.		
Tithing is not important.		
Tip God occasionally.		
Leave wealth for your children.		
Be generous to others.		
Give to the poor.		
Emotional		
Everybody has feelings.		
Feelings are truth.		
Obey all your feelings.		
Evaluate feelings, but don't decide with them.		
Your feelings are important.		
Your feelings are not important.		
It's easy to talk about feelings.		
It's hard to talk about feelings.		

Table 4-4: Attitudes and Beliefs Modeled by My Parents

	Mother	Father
We just don't talk about feelings.		
Handling conflict		
Every battle is a war.		
No conflict is bigger than our love for each other.		
Fight dirty, just win.		
Conflict is about dominance.		
Bring up the past.		
Shame the person to discredit their ideas.		
Conflict is about discovering the best idea.		
Don't fight.		
When you run out of ideas, use anger.		
You're not accountable if you were angry.		
Make up quickly after the conflict.		
Hold grudges.		
Punish by silence.		

Table 4-4: Attitudes and Beliefs Modeled by My Parents		
	Mother	**Father**
Punish by being passive.		
Make them pay.		
I have to be right.		
I have to look good.		
I can't have bad motives or ideas.		
The other person is always selfish.		
Push buttons to watch them get out of control to avoid the real issue.		
When you lose, don't admit it.		
Compromise is acceptable.		
Sometimes others have better ideas.		
I have no value if I'm not right.		
Morality		
Rules are for everyone.		
We are all accountable to God.		
We are only accountable to ourselves.		

Table 4-4: Attitudes and Beliefs Modeled by My Parents

	Mother	Father
Only you know if something is right or wrong.		
Cheating is never OK.		
Lying is never OK.		
It's OK to lie or cheat.		
Rules are for fools.		
I'm smarter, so I don't have to obey the rules.		
There is no such thing as a secret.		
You always pay for wrong decisions.		
Cheating, lying, stealing, or being immoral is only wrong if caught.		
There is no connection between moral decisions and your faith in God.		
Right is always right.		
Wrong is always wrong.		
Nobody knows what's really right or wrong.		
Marriage		
Love your spouse.		

Table 4-4: Attitudes and Beliefs Modeled by My Parents

	Mother	Father
Always be faithful.		
Expose their weakness.		
Shame them.		
Control them.		
Men are more important than women.		
Bully your spouse.		
Build up your spouse.		
Make time for the marriage.		
Have resources to date.		
Give gifts to your spouse.		
Be affectionate toward your spouse.		
Don't be affectionate to your spouse.		
He who makes more money is important.		
One spouse really makes the decisions.		

I think as you evaluate the attitudes and beliefs of your parents, you will get a sense of where some of your ideas and beliefs may have developed. Some of what you may have gleaned from your parents was good. Others may have gleaned some pretty bad ideas and beliefs that greatly impacted their future beliefs and behaviors.

Again, the purpose of reviewing these beliefs and attitudes is not to use the information to blame anyone. Blaming does not move you toward change. Your choice to duplicate a modeled behavior is still yours. The fact that your parents were not educated about certain behaviors or beliefs does not stop you from becoming educated in order to handle things in healthier ways. If they didn't save and invest, that doesn't stop you from saving and investing your money. You can get a grip on the things that control you if, rather than blaming or looking for excuses, you put in place proven strategies for success.

This journey of researching where behaviors have come from can be painful and thought provoking. This is not where the journey ends, though. The journey you are about to embark upon is one filled with hope. I have seen so many people get a grip on what was controlling them that it actually motivates me to show up weekly to see it happen again in my counseling practice.

It may surprise you to know that I have personally experienced most of the cities of origin for out-of-control behavior. I have experienced abandonment, abuse, shame, and poor role models, but I also have learned how to get a grip on many things in my life that had control of me.

Almost anyone willing to do the work outlined in these future chapters can get control of what is controlling them. I wish you a great journey as you continue to learn how to get a grip on what is controlling you.

Chapter Five

Scapegoats, Victim Mentalities, and Other Myths

"Somebody's gonna pay!" exclaims the boss, and everybody on the floor knows what that means. The boss got in trouble for something, so he is going to find someone to pin it on; that person will now be the scapegoat for the problem so the boss can look wonderful again. It is amazing how we look for scapegoats in our lives so we can look good.

I think the human race has a fundamental flaw in its processing when it comes to blaming others. We honestly believe we are to preserve our own reputation at the expense of everyone else. I have no idea how most of us believe in this, but it is prevalent everywhere. From the student who forgot his homework but swears it was "his roommate's fault" or "the computer's fault" to the parent who blames some other child in the neighborhood for their own child's misbehavior. This is nothing new; it goes all the way back to Adam and Eve. Let's read a few scriptures to illustrate this funny part of our human nature. Let me set the scene here.

The snake talks to Eve. Eve eats the apple. She gives it to Adam. Adam eats the apple. Remember, this was the only thing their heavenly Father said not to do. So what did they both do? Eat the apple. Listen in on the dialogue after this misbehavior.

> And he [God] said, "Who told you that you were naked? Have you eaten from the tree that I commanded you not to eat from?"
>
> The man said, "The woman you put here with me—she gave me some fruit from the tree, and I ate it."
>
> Then the LORD God said to the woman, "What is this you have done?"
>
> The woman said, "The serpent deceived me, and I ate."
>
> —GENESIS 3:11–13

So you can see Adam scapegoats Eve, and Eve scapegoats the serpent. Who knows what would have happened if Adam would have just said, "I am fully responsible for myself, and I ask Your forgiveness."

What if Eve would have just said, "I am responsible for listening to the serpent, lusting in my heart, and sinning against You, and then inviting Adam into the same sin. I'm sorry, Father; please forgive me!"

Maybe the consequence would have been the same; it is hard to say. But at least maybe this scapegoat thing would have not been passed down from the very beginning.

Right now, I am sitting in an airport (again), and in the last hour, with only the people sitting around me, I have heard more than once, "It's not my fault." "Don't blame me." "It was ____________ 's fault."

It really is amazing how much this type of thinking infiltrates our day-to-day lives. Take a moment to reflect on your last conversation with your spouse, children, or other family members. How many times have you said or heard, "It's not my fault" or other versions of this lack of responsibility for behavior? The number might surprise you.

I think it will be helpful to go through some of the major scapegoats that we humans utilize to explain our out-of-control behavior. This can help us move through some of the blocks that have kept us from getting a grip on what has been controlling our lives.

God

It may or may not come as a surprise to you, but many people blame God for their out-of-control behavior. Have you ever seen T-shirts that say "Born to shop" or "Born to eat chocolate"? I know we all laugh at these sayings, but unfortunately there are some who actually believe that God Himself bears the responsibility for the out-of-control areas of our lives, that we were just "born that way" and there's nothing we can do about it. Let's look at a scripture that clears this up for us.

> When tempted, no one should say, "God is tempting me." For God cannot be tempted by evil, nor does he tempt anyone; but each one is tempted when, by his own evil desire, he is dragged away and enticed.
>
> —James 1:13–14

Clearly God does not tempt us to eat, have sex, or work inappropriately. He does not cause us to become angry, self-righteous, envious, self-absorbed, prideful, reckless, unkind, or controlled by any other behavior.

God created us in His image. He created us to be loving, kind, patient, understanding, creative, fun, nurturing, and all of His other wonderful characteristics. He created us without sin or even an appetite for sin. We were created absolutely pure and sinless. I mean, Adam did not even know he was naked—that's pretty pure!

So God did not create us for whatever is controlling us. It is not His design at all that we continue to use our minds, our will, our emotions, and our bodies in a submissive manner to whatever is controlling us. Often it pains Him to see us being limited by behaviors that have control over us. He cries at our being limited.

Many think that God is an angry God. But He is really more compassionate, similar to what a parent would be. As a parent you can see a behavior like slothfulness or procrastination in your child. You try everything you can to help your child move from slothful to becoming motivated and industrious. Year after year you ache about this slothful behavior. You may get upset at times, but at a deeper level you hurt for this child because you know that slothfulness has control over him and will eventually limit his quality of life, friendships, marriage, and parenting, as well as other areas of his life.

That is how God feels about what is controlling your life. He may get upset at times, but His deeper feeling toward you is sadness because this will handicap you, your friendships, marriage, and parenting.

Suppose your out-of-control behavior is envy. You envy those who are richer, more important, more beautiful, skinnier, and happier. God is sad because you are not able to celebrate the wonder of you that He created. He is sad because your friendships will be limited and your ability to trust and connect to these "more wonderful" people will be limited. Your mate will suffer the entire marriage because you cannot be happy with who you are and how good your life really is. Your children will have undue stress to measure up and then wonder why they cannot be like so-and-so.

Rather than making God your scapegoat or thinking that He has no compassion for what you are going through, realize that God can be an ally to help you get a grip on what has been controlling you. He is your biggest cheerleader. If you could hear Him, He would be saying, "Get up, and try again. Keep going. I am so proud of you."

The devil

Now since we cannot blame the "good guy in the sky," who's left? Many people find a bad guy to blame for their out-of-control behavior. Yes, you know who I mean—the devil. I think we all have seen T-shirts, bumper stickers, or heard people say, "The devil made me do it."

I have been counseling people for almost two decades, so you can trust me when I say that the devil is a popular scapegoat. I have heard the devil blamed for adultery, pornography, greed, embezzlement, fear, poor decisions—all the way down to the cupcake binge. I have heard countless people blame the devil for situations in which owning up to their personal responsibility would have been a much better idea.

Perhaps you have heard someone say, "If you're not part of the solution, you're part of the problem." People say this to point out that if we see a problem in our lives, our families, our churches, or our communities, but we don't do anything to change it, our inaction makes us part of the problem. After counseling many people who do not take responsibility for their problems, I have created my own version of this saying. I like to say: *If you are not the problem, then you are not the solution.*

Let me explain. If a couple comes in for counseling and the man blames the wife for all the problems, then he has no ability to be a solution since he is not the problem. But if he can see his own part of the problem, then he can become the solution for that part of the problem.

If "the devil is the problem," then as a counselor I am really stuck. That means that the devil has all the power to be the solution. I would have to dial up the devil and ask him to stop bothering my client in order for my client to improve. We all know that the devil has not been taking calls to help people improve their lives lately, so I would be on hold indefinitely, and my client, the "victim of the devil," would be unable to change.

I think you clearly know where I am going. If I blame the devil, I am making myself unable to be the solution. The story goes something like this: The devil (over whom I, as a believer, have been given authority through Christ) tempts or influences me to do my out-of-control behavior again. The devil (whom Christ within me is stronger than) "makes me do it."

Let's come to an understanding about the devil. He is a singular being. That means he, like a human, can only be at one place at one time. He is not omnipresent like God; he cannot be everywhere all the time. The devil is a limited being in time and space like all of us.

If the devil is in Chicago, he can only be in Chicago. He cannot be in LA, New York, Boston, or Washington DC at the same time.

He would have to be pretty fast to be tempting my telephone clients in Baton Rouge and Seattle within twenty minutes of each other! Somehow I just do not think that happens. If the real devil with all of his hate, fear, and fallen beauty-turned-into-ugliness came walking into your kitchen, you wouldn't be able to eat that cupcake, commit adultery, look at pornography, or anything else to save your life. You would be screaming, crying, and begging to get as far away from him as possible.

So you see, the devil probably isn't a legitimate scapegoat for any out-of-control behavior. Remember, *if you are not the problem, you are not the solution.* When you are the problem, you are the solution.

Now, some of you Bible scholars might want to blame some of the angels that fell from heaven with the devil—you know, the demons. Demons are real, but you still choose your behaviors. Hear my heart; I know there are spiritual influences, just as there are other influences that affect your behavior, but ultimately, barring severe psychological disorders, you have to choose to conduct—or not to conduct—any behavior. Also, if Christ dwelling in you gives you power to overcome the devil, certainly you can use the authority you have in Christ to successfully ward off a few of his imps.

The flesh

Remember our story about Adam and Eve? You know, eating the apple and all that? Well, since then we as humans have had a tendency toward less-than-wonderful behavior. We call this a *sinful nature* in religious terms. It is that urge inside all of us that says, "Go for it," when we think of doing something we know that we should not do.

Maybe this story about a recent trip I made from Colorado Springs to Pittsburgh will help you to understand what I mean. The day of my trip, I arose early to catch my flight. I called the airline to make sure the seating was to my liking and learned that I had great seats all the way to Pittsburgh. I would be flying from

Colorado Springs to Denver, where I would grab a connecting flight to Pittsburgh. Perfect. I arrived at the airport in plenty of time for my 8:00 a.m. flight and found the second closest parking space to the airport entrance. I breezed through check-in and security and made my way to the gate. Everything was going smoothly. *This is going to be a great trip,* I said, smiling to myself. *Maybe I'll even have time to work on my book while I'm traveling.*

That's when this happy, carefree story took a turn for the worse. At the gate, I was told that they couldn't get our plane to start, but they would keep trying. Let me insert here that traveling from Colorado Springs to Denver takes a mere fifteen minutes by plane and only one hour by car. After a slight delay, I was told that I was placed on the next flight at 9:00 a.m., and I would still have enough time to make my connection.

In a few minutes I found myself, along with several other inconvenienced passengers, being loaded up for a 9:00 a.m. flight. I was getting concerned I wouldn't be able to eat breakfast in Denver as planned, but I decided to make the best of it.

As I sat on the 9:00 a.m. plane contemplating my lost morning meal, the pilot announced that they were having "technical difficulties." My patience grew thinner and thinner as the time grew later and later.

Finally, we took off, but instead of a fifteen-minute "hop" to Denver, I noticed that our plane flew over Denver, and then north of Denver, which was far out of the way for this type of flight. (I knew this from having flown to Denver to connect to other flights many times before.) We circled around and finally landed, but that left me with only minutes to get to another gate. At least I could still look forward to that great seat assignment I would have on the flight to Pittsburgh.

I checked my ticket for the gate number. I was at gate 61 and the flight to Pittsburgh departed from gate…22! As I ran from one end of the airport to the other, I didn't even have time to think about how far I was running. All I wanted to do was get in that great seat on the plane and relax all the way to Pittsburgh.

I arrived at gate 22, panting, only to find that the door was closed. I showed the gate attendant my ticket. "You're not on this United flight," she said. "Your ticket is United, but you are on a different carrier and that plane left twenty minutes ago." Right then, my sinful nature wanted to rise up and start "explaining" my situation. Fortunately the flight attendant was kind and boarded me on the last seat of the plane anyway.

I was relieved to make the flight, but as for my wonderful seat...you guessed it. It was on the plane that had left twenty minutes ago! Instead, I was stuck in a middle seat with two big, burly men on either side of me. My sinful nature wanted to tell the airline staff exactly how much they had ruined my perfectly planned trip, and yet, I chose to be grateful to have been placed on the flight at all.

That thing that rises up inside of us that wants to yell, scream, pout, manipulate, impress, bully, or demean others is our sinful nature, which is also called our *flesh*. It can be hard to explain, but you definitely know when it shows up. How many of us have been at a store or restaurant when someone starts to go off on a clerk or server. How many of us have been guilty of the same thing? The flesh usually stinks when it shows up. It is ugly. It is what happens when someone or something "brings out the worst" in us. It is our sinful nature, and it wants to get its own way or make others pay.

But we need to remember that our sinful nature or flesh is ours to control. We cannot use our flesh as a scapegoat; God's Word tells us that we have to kill our fleshly desires every day. It is our responsibility. We can choose to speak a kind answer to someone trying to help in a situation, or we can be as unkind as our flesh wants us to be. We can choose to look at magazines, videos, or television programs that we know are ungodly, or we can choose to look away and remove ourselves from the situation.

Conquering the flesh is hard, but it is still our choice. I know this radical idea of being responsible flies in the face of a victim mantra our culture exposes through the media and through politicians, but they are just wrong. I am 100 percent responsible for my choices—good or bad, kind or unkind, patient or impatient, fleshy or spiritual. They are all *my* choices. The same goes for everyone.

Bad ideas

Another scapegoat that can be utilized by those who have an out-of-control behavior is bad ideas. Our culture—and every other culture, for that matter—is full of ideas. Since humans generate these ideas, they can range from really good ideas all the way to really bad ones.

Let's look at ideas about marriage. There is the idea that marriage is between one man and one woman for life, exclusive of all others. Then there is the idea that cheating on your spouse is acceptable. Then there is the idea that you can keep divorcing and remarrying until you find Mr. or Mrs. Right.

How about parenting ideas? There is an idea that parents should raise their own children. There is also an idea that the government should raise our children. There are different ideas on how to discipline children, educate them, feed them, nurture them—the list is seemingly endless.

Even the church is full of great and not-so-great ideas. There is an idea that we should serve others, and there is the idea we should exploit others' needs. There is the idea we should love others and the idea we should judge them.

Ideas are everywhere around us. Healthy ideas are like our vegetables; if we eat them, they are good for us and give us a healthier life. Bad ideas are the junk foods; they look like food, but a regular diet of them can cause terrible damage to ourselves and to those around us.

Ideas are important because our ideas shape our behaviors. My wife, Lisa, has this idea that she only needs to eat what she will actually utilize that day. This is a good idea that produces behaviors like eating meat selectively, not eating late at night (hot tea only), and minimal desserts. This behavior has caused Lisa to stay in the same size clothing and not gain any weight during the twenty-five years that I have known her.

I, on the other hand, have the idea of eating almost anything and celebrating with food. This causes behaviors of eating unnecessary desserts, not regulating my intake on any regular basis, and if I want a snack at night, I almost feel entitled to eat one. My bad ideas have caused me, shall we say, *not* to weigh the same as when we met.

Can you see how Lisa's idea produced behavior that in turn produced a certain lifestyle? How about mine? This is true for all of us. Our ideas affect our behavior, and the way we behave over time becomes our lifestyle. This lifestyle of repeated behaviors ultimately determines the destiny of our relationships. That's right—the quality of our lifelong relationships begins with the ideas we allow to shape our behaviors.

To help explain what I mean, let's investigate what life might be like for a person who chooses to believe an idea of entitlement to be angry toward people. He has experienced something painful, so he believes he is entitled to give pain away to others at whim. The person who chooses this idea will be explosive, easily frustrated, and will demand that others serve him, or he'll "make them pay" with some chiding outburst. This person will damage his spouse, children, co-workers, and neighbors, and will usually end up alone at the end of his life.

However, when a person who has been given pain decides to believe the idea that he is 100 percent responsible to heal from this pain and that he should try not to give pain to others as much as possible, he experiences the opposite results in his lifestyle and relationships. The person who chooses this idea will not be prone to outbursts or controlling others but will exercise patience with other people. He will be kind to his spouse, children, co-workers, and neighbors. At the end of his life, he is more likely to have friends and be loved by those who are significant to him.

Evaluating our ideas is insightful as we get a grip on what is controlling us. Like God, the devil, and the flesh, ideas are at our disposal. We can choose an idea of entitlement for our out-of-control behavior, or we can choose other ideas that can help us. We can try to blame bad ideas or use them as a scapegoat for our out-of-control behavior, but the truth is that our ideas should be our servants, and we have the power to be the masters of them.

The bottom line is that there are no scapegoats. I alone choose to comply with the ideas or influences that support my out-of-control behavior. The same is true for everyone. I know this is hard to digest if you have been eating the cultural diet that tells you your behavior is somebody else's fault or you are a victim of something and that is why you behave the way you do.

Trust me, I am not an insensitive clod who doesn't understand pain. I was conceived in adultery, abandoned by a dad I never met and a mother who placed me in foster homes. I have been abused, addicted, and so on. I am familiar with pain, but pain is not an excuse; it is an identifier of where I need to heal in order to improve my quality of life and the lives of those who will be touched by me in some way.

You see, in my life, after visiting the cities of abandonment and abuse, after rounds of blaming God, the devil, the flesh, and bad ideas, I had to take a hard look at who was really responsible for my out-of-control behaviors. What I discovered was that anything that had control over me was 100 percent my responsibility.

It was I who had chosen to use my past, my flesh, my bad ideas, and my negative spiritual influences as an excuse. But I had to realize that these things did not force me into a certain behavior or belief. I chose to think and act the way I did. I alone was—and still am—responsible for me.

IT'S YOUR TURN TO TAKE RESPONSIBILITY

Now it's your turn. Try saying it aloud: "I am 100 percent responsible for me." How do you feel when you say this? Take a moment and write down your honest feelings.

Taking responsibility makes me feel ______________________

____.

Some people get really angry at this point. Others become sad when they realize how they have been duped into scapegoating. Others report relief, as if they now have a diagnosis that can lead them to new answers.

Check your body as well. How does your body feel when you say, "I am 100 percent responsible for me"? Take a moment and write this down as well.

Taking responsibility makes my body feel __________________

____.

Some report a certain uncomfortable feeling. Others report feeling uptight, and still others relaxed. Your body can sometimes tell you how something really settles with you.

Now let's take it one step further. You are responsible for the choices you make—good or bad. You are responsible for your behavior. Now I want you to say aloud, "I am 100 percent responsible for my out-of-control behavior."

Now say it again, naming the specific behavior or behaviors in your situation. For example, if you are dealing with acting superior to others, you need to say, "I am 100 percent responsible for my out-of-control behavior of acting superior to others." All right, try saying this aloud about your out-of-control behavior.

Now take a second and check your feelings. How do you feel when you say you are 100 percent responsible for your behavior? In my experience, people often experience an amplification of the earlier feelings at this point. If you felt angry, confused, or relieved in taking responsibility for yourself, you tend to feel more of that when you speak it out loud that you are 100 percent responsible for your out-of-control behavior. Use the space provided to record how you feel right now.

Taking responsibility for my behavior made me feel:

____

____.

Also check your body. How does your body feel when you say, "I am 100 percent responsible for my out-of-control behavior"? Again it may be an amplification of what you previously experienced in saying "I am 100 percent responsible for me." Jot it down in the space provided.

Taking responsibility for my behavior made my body feel:

____

____.

By now you probably have a good idea of how you feel about being 100 percent responsible for you. Whether you are angry, confused, or lost, you can move to a place of relief. I've known many clients who found this type of relief once they identified exactly what their problem was and took responsibility for it.

Juan was such a client. He grew up in sunny California with a single mother. When he came to see me he was thirty-two and struggling in his career and in his marriage. He reported not having any "get up and go." He was getting to work late because he wanted to sleep. He felt worthless and had difficulty concentrating and making decisions. He also reported gaining twenty-five pounds in the last six months.

When I explained to Juan that he was clinically depressed, I read the criteria right out of the diagnostic manual. He sat back in his chair and said, "Thank God!"

I was confused and asked, "You are thanking God that you are depressed?"

"No, no!" he replied. "I'm thanking God there is a name for what I'm going through!"

Once Juan had the diagnosis, he took responsibility for clinical and medical approaches to get out of the depression. He did great in therapy and feels healthier without the weight and the feeling of being depressed all the time. His wife, Carmen, was also very happy.

Hopefully you are already at a place of being relieved that you found the problem, or you can see that you are on your way to that place of relief. It may help you to remember: *if you are the problem, you are the solution.*

I personally love being the problem. When I am the problem, I know I am the solution. I will involve God and others in the solution, but I am responsible for the solution. So, congratulations; you are the problem *and* you are your solution!

Now that you have identified yourself as the problem, the next step on our journey is identifying and learning to cope with the emotions you are probably cycling through as a result of your out-of-control behavior.

PART 3

Getting a Grip on Out-of-Control Behavior

Get A GRIP

Chapter Six

Step 1: Self-Honesty

Carol was a twenty-eight-year-old mother of two. She was bright but very overwhelmed with her role as a mother and part-time bookkeeper for her father's company. Her husband was finishing his master's degree while working forty hours a week in a local psychiatric hospital with his shifts rotating between the middle and late shift.

Needless to say, anyone would empathize with this difficult stage of life. Carol also had a history of bulimia. When she was in her late teens and early twenties, she became so plagued with this behavior she spent some time in a treatment center.

As you might guess with the stress she was experiencing as a mother in her late twenties, she was falling back to her old patterns of binge-eating and purging. She was eating to deal with her stress, but she did not want any further weight gain after having her two children. She already didn't like her body with the added weight. In her mind this was overwhelming.

For more than eight months Carol had been secretly eating cakes, cookies, pizza, and other large quantities of food, and then purging—sometimes twice a day. She felt totally out of control. But in order to change, she would have to face a big turning point.

Lance was a really good guy. He was forty and fun to be with. He had three great sons, and his wife, Heidi, was a schoolteacher and a Sunday school teacher at their local Nazarene church. Lance was quick to help his friends, his neighbors, and his church. He was successful as an insurance company salesperson and well-liked by his peers.

However, Lance had an area of his life that was totally out of control. He had an Internet problem. No, he was not looking at pornography or going into chat rooms. His problem was Internet investing. He woke up early to check the markets. He followed the market throughout the day and sometimes even spent his lunch break at his desk so that he could check the market.

It all started when, after Heidi agreed, Lance withdrew the $10,000 they had been saving and put it toward investing. He made some good hits in his first few weeks, taking the $10,000 to $18,000. Both Heidi and Lance were happy, and Heidi pretty much left Lance alone, "since he knew what he was doing."

Unfortunately, Lance did *not* know what he was doing, and before long, the $18,000 was gone. Lance couldn't bear to tell Heidi. So he started doing more investing to cover his stock market losses, and after a few months he found himself $83,000 in debt. He kept it a secret, using commission checks from the office. He also took a $10,000 advance and took $15,000 out of their 401K without Heidi knowing.

Lance was filled with anxiety. He hated what he had done, and yet he was still addicted to watching the market. He was out of control by anyone's standards. Lance had to face a turning point.

The turning point for both Carol and Lance is the turning point for anyone who has out-of-control behavior. You must be honest—not just honest, but *brutally honest*—with yourself about your behavior. This can be tough, especially if you recall that denial, anger, and rationalization are all part of the cycle of out-of-control behavior. I have found that honesty is the very first step to becoming the solution.

When I was working in an alcohol and drug treatment center, we went through this process every week with individuals whose alcohol or drug usage landed them in the hospital. They were in the center because they either had a job- or marriage-threatening event, and yet they could not take this first step of self-honesty during the first few days of their treatment.

We would hear the classic, "I don't drink that much. Everyone should be able to have a beer. One mistake doesn't make a drunk." They actually believed these statements as they sat in a chair in a psychiatric hospital surrounded by other alcoholics. It was amazing to me to regularly see the state of self-deception of these individuals who had obviously experienced out-of-control behavior.

However, with most cases, *something* happened, something that brought about the turning point in people's lives. For one alcoholic man in denial named Fred, his *something* could only be explained as miraculous. One day in a group session, Fred was confronted—not by the therapist, but by his peers.

One by one they tore down his self-deception. They were motivated by love and Fred's betterment. They were not getting paid to care, neither did they have to worry about saying the right thing.

As Fred was repeatedly confronted about his true condition, you could see his position weaken until it happened—a moment of clarity. He was able to see that he really was an alcoholic.

Fred had been lying to himself, and it was amazing to watch as Fred's eyes cleared up. It was as if a veil was taken off his eyes, and he could now see himself and his life with clarity. Fred experienced self-honesty—the gift of having an honest opinion of yourself.

For change to occur, you must first look at yourself and honestly admit what you see. If you do not admit the problem to yourself, you cannot change. You truly cannot change what you don't see as wrong or needing to change. You will simply continue to repeat the cycle of out-of-control behavior—denial, anger, rationalization, sadness, motivation, hopelessness—but you will not change.

For eight months, Carol could not change. "It's just a phase. I'm not really sick again." For months, Lance could not change. He was so busy covering up his out-of-control behavior that all he could do was assure himself that the next trade would make it better, and then he would put it all back.

Both Carol and Lance had a moment of clarity, a moment of self-honesty. For Carol, the moment came when she passed out in a restroom while forcing herself to purge. Her three-year-old found her and cried until Carol came to.

The situation forced her to think about how long she had been unconscious and what might happen to her beautiful children if this occurred again. She had to say within her, "I'm out of control." Thankfully, Carol admitted that she had a problem and sought help the next day to get a grip on what was controlling her.

Lance's honesty was slightly different. Heidi received a call from the bank that their line of credit for $30,000 was approved. She knew the banker and asked him when Lance requested this. She picked up the papers at the bank and had the children sent to Grandma's house for the night. When Lance came home, they had what some might call a "come to Jesus" meeting.

Heidi's rage at being kept in the dark about their finances, her persistence about what the credit was for, and her demands to see what he was doing in his trade "business" lasted for hours. Lance slowly gave bits and pieces of information that led to Heidi's crying and weeping about what had been going on.

Lance was finally able to see what he had done and was able to admit, "I have a problem." He wasn't open to help right away, but Heidi's strong encouragement prompted Lance to seek help and really experience the turning point of self-honesty that he desperately needed to help him take the first step toward getting a grip.

TWO PATHS TO HUMILITY

Self-honesty is your first step out of the cycle of out-of-control behavior, but there are two different paths people take to reach this point. I often tell my clients, "There are two paths to humility." The first path to humility is to humble yourself. This is where you just choose to be honest about a flaw in your life. You humble yourself and admit to you exactly what is true. Self-honesty is by far the easier of the two paths to humility.

The second path is definitely the harder path. In this path you stay in denial, anger, and rationalization, and you keep the out-of-control behavior protected from honesty. Then *something* happens—negative consequences, some form of exposure, or what I call a "God moment" occurs and you reach your turning point.

For many, this moment is the moment when they are absolutely caught. Their spouse, friends, children, church members, and maybe even the entire community find out about their out-of-control behavior. This path to humility is more accurately called *humiliation!* Someone has been embarrassed by his or her own behavior, and now he or she has little choice but to be humble. This humility is much more painful. It hurts when you are humiliated, and it often takes years to rebuild your life.

As a counselor with years of experience, I have seen people take both paths. I have seen men and women who honestly face up to their out-of-control behavior and seek help. They integrate the principles in this book, and they move on with their lives. It does not take long for them to see their progress and experience happier, healthier lives.

But I also see men and women who have had to suffer public humiliation due to a lack of self-honesty. People who choose this path have a much harder and longer road to happiness. They not only have to get a grip on the area that is controlling them, but they also have to deal with the humiliation and other consequences of having their behavior exposed to others.

These consequences might include a damaged spousal relationship, damaged relationships with their children, co-workers, church friends, and damaged ministry and outreach efforts. There might be financial consequences from which it can take a season of time to recover, especially if there is a loss of job involved. Some behaviors cause legal issues as well.

Take another look at Lance's situation. Stopping the trading was actually easier overall than rebuilding trust with Heidi. On top of that, he had to explain to their children why they were not doing the annual all-inclusive ski vacation. He didn't have to file for bankruptcy, but he did have to go through a process of financing the entire $83,000. Then he had to go to his boss with Heidi and explain his humiliating situation. They arranged that all bonuses be directly applied to their newly acquired second mortgage.

Lance did not travel the road through humiliation as quickly as someone who humbles himself. However, Lance was able to pay off his debt in two and a half years and restore his relationship with his wife and family. He was so much more focused and productive at work that he actually was salesman of the year during the second year of his restoration. His boss, wife, children, and pastor were all proud of the way Lance handled himself through the whole process with his out-of-control behavior. He has earned the trust back from those who are closest to him.

Why did I tell you the two paths to humility? Because in the days ahead you are going to make one of the most important decisions of your life. That decision is to be honest with yourself.

YOU ARE HURTING YOURSELF

If you were honest with yourself as you read through the previous chapters, you probably discovered one or more out-of-control behaviors in your life. I have always found it very beneficial for my clients to write things down, so I encourage you to write down each area that you believe is out of control. For each behavior that you list in the space on the next page, I want you to write how this behavior is hurting you.

Table 6-1: How My Out-of-Control Behavior Hurts Me

Behavior 1 ____________________

How this behavior is hurting me:

____

____

____

____

Behavior 2 ____________________

How this behavior is hurting me:

____

____

____

____

Behavior 3 ____________________

How this behavior is hurting me:

____

____

____

____

Behavior 4 ____________________

How this behavior is hurting me:

____

Behavior 5 ____________________

How this behavior is hurting me:

Behavior 6 ____________________

How this behavior is hurting me:

Behavior 7 ____________________

How this behavior is hurting me:

Behavior 8 ____________________

How this behavior is hurting me:

Behavior 9 ____________________

How this behavior is hurting me:

Behavior 10 ____________________

How this behavior is hurting me:

ARE YOU HURTING OTHERS?

There may be a few out-of-control behaviors that have only hurt you and no one else, but that is a rare instance. People who overeat might naïvely believe that it only affects them, but that is denial. The fact is, it really does affect their families when they cannot participate in typical family activities such as hiking or bike riding. Their business relationships can be impacted by the health conditions that are likely to accompany obesity, and their larger size can even affect those around them when seated during travel, sports games, or other events. Perhaps no one says anything out of politeness or rationalization, but the person with out-of-control behavior impacts even innocent bystanders. Allow me to illustrate my point.

As I write this, I am sitting as comfortably as one possibly can in the O'Hare International Airport in Chicago. The gentleman next to me is on his cell phone. He sounds enraged. I can't even write what he is saying. He is so angry that this wing of the airport has no smoking areas. He will have to go out of the airport and come back through security if he wants to smoke a cigarette. He is going on and on about having a one-and-a-half-hour layover and not being able to have a cigarette.

Here I am, a total stranger, being affected by two of this man's out-of-control behaviors—nicotine addiction and anger. I am sure both of these are impacting his marriage, children, employment, and other areas of his life. I pray that he has a great day, but I doubt he will ever know how his out-of-control behavior impacted a stranger in an airport.

I tell you this to illustrate that most of your out-of-control behaviors impact others in your life. In the space provided list those you believe are being impacted by the out-of-control behavior you listed previously.

Table 6-2: Whom Does My Out-of-Control Behavior Affect?

Behavior 1 ______________________________

People being impacted by my out-of-control behavior are:

1. ____________	5. ____________
2. ____________	6. ____________
3. ____________	7. ____________
4. ____________	8. ____________

Behavior 2 ______________________________

People being impacted by my out-of-control behavior are:

1. ______________ 5. ______________

2. ______________ 6. ______________

3. ______________ 7. ______________

4. ______________ 8. ______________

Behavior 3 ______________________________

People being impacted by my out-of-control behavior are:

1. ______________ 5. ______________

2. ______________ 6. ______________

3. ______________ 7. ______________

4. ______________ 8. ______________

Behavior 4 ______________________________

People being impacted by my out-of-control behavior are:

1. ______________ 5. ______________

2. ______________ 6. ______________

3. ______________ 7. ______________

4. ______________ 8. ______________

Behavior 5 ______________________________

People being impacted by my out-of-control behavior are:

1. ______________ 5. ______________

2. ______________ 6. ______________

3. ______________ 7. ______________

4. ______________________ 8. ______________________

Behavior 6 ____

People being impacted by my out-of-control behavior are:

1. ______________________ 5. ______________________

2. ______________________ 6. ______________________

3. ______________________ 7. ______________________

4. ______________________ 8. ______________________

Behavior 7 ____

People being impacted by my out-of-control behavior are:

1. ______________________ 5. ______________________

2. ______________________ 6. ______________________

3. ______________________ 7. ______________________

4. ______________________ 8. ______________________

Behavior 8 ____

People being impacted by my out-of-control behavior are:

1. ______________________ 5. ______________________

2. ______________________ 6. ______________________

3. ______________________ 7. ______________________

4. ______________________ 8. ______________________

Behavior 9 ____

People being impacted by my out-of-control behavior are:

1. ______________________ 5. ______________________

2. ______________________ 6. ______________________

3. ______________ 7. ______________

4. ______________ 8. ______________

Behavior 10 ______________________________

People being impacted by my out-of-control behavior are:

1. ______________ 5. ______________

2. ______________ 6. ______________

3. ______________ 7. ______________

4. ______________ 8. ______________

If you begin to regress into denial or rationalization of your out-of-control behavior, what you write can be helpful. You can read your own writing about how this out-of-control behavior has hurt you and others and become awakened again to the realization you had at this sober moment in your life. Similar to when Fred's eyes cleared up, you might need a written record this time to clear your eyes in the future.

So I encourage you not to skip over this step in your turning point. This exercise in honesty is the first step of change in gaining control over what has been controlling you. In the space provided, write a summary of how this out-of-control behavior is hurting those you listed earlier.

Table 6-3: How My Out-of-Control Behavior Hurts Others

Behavior 1 ______________________________

How this behavior is hurting others:

____

____

Behavior 2 ____________________

How this behavior is hurting others:

Behavior 3 ____________________

How this behavior is hurting others:

Behavior 4 ____________________

How this behavior is hurting others:

Behavior 5 ____________________

How this behavior is hurting others:

Behavior 6 ____________________

How this behavior is hurting others:

Behavior 7 ____________________

How this behavior is hurting others:

Behavior 8 ____________________

How this behavior is hurting others:

Behavior 9 ____________________

How this behavior is hurting others:

Behavior 10 __________

How this behavior is hurting others:

I think by now you are getting a handle on the concept of self-honesty. I know it can be difficult to see yourself in this manner, but once you can see the impact you are having on your life and the lives of others you love, it becomes difficult to deny, become angry, or rationalize the continuation of the out-of-control behavior.

ARE YOU HURTING GOD'S HEART?

Now, I want to take you into another relationship that you may not have included in your list of people who have been impacted by your out-of-control behavior. That relationship is the one you have with God.

You see, God is a person. He has a heart with feelings and perceptions about your behavior, especially your out-of-control behavior. God watches you and me when we are controlled by His Spirit, and He also watches us when our out-of-control behavior controls us.

I know we somehow try to block our awareness of how these behaviors affect the very heart and person of the living God. So I want us to go there just for a moment.

In the space provided write down how your out-of-control behavior impacts God. You can also write how this out-of-control behavior impacts your relationship with Him.

Table 6-4: How My Out-of-Control Behavior Hurts God

Behavior 1 ____

How my out-of-control behavior impacts the heart and person of God:

____

____

____

____

Behavior 2 ____

How my out-of-control behavior impacts the heart and person of God:

____

____

____

____

Behavior 3 ____

How my out-of-control behavior impacts the heart and person of God:

____

____

____

Behavior 4 ______

How my out-of-control behavior impacts the heart and person of God:

Behavior 5 ______

How my out-of-control behavior impacts the heart and person of God:

Behavior 6 ______

How my out-of-control behavior impacts the heart and person of God:

Behavior 7 ______

How my out-of-control behavior impacts the heart and person of God:

____

____

Behavior 8 __________________________________

How my out-of-control behavior impacts the heart and person of God:

____

____

____

____

Behavior 9 __________________________________

How my out-of-control behavior impacts the heart and person of God:

____

____

____

____

Behavior 10 __________________________________

How my out-of-control behavior impacts the heart and person of God:

____

____

____

____

Wow, now you are really being honest! How do you feel? Drained? Insightful? Sober? Committed? Hopeful? My clients report all these feelings and more when they have reached the turning point you have just experienced.

I know you can feel overwhelmed by these behaviors that have been running your life. Don't worry, that's temporary. You have faced your turning point, and you can now walk out of the cycle of out-of-control behavior and, through your honesty, continue your journey to get a grip on what is controlling you.

During my training as a counselor, I spent thousands of hours with alcohol and drug addicts. I learned a lot during that time about getting control of the things that control you. One of the most important concepts I remember is that the first step is often the longest one to get to and the hardest one to climb. It may have taken you years to become honest, really honest with your out-of-control behavior, but now that you've jumped the biggest hurdle, rest assured that you can finish the journey.

Take a minute and imagine what your life would look like without this out-of-control behavior. Actually, do more than just think about it; write it down. In the space below or on a separate piece of paper, write how your life would be different if this out-of-control behavior was not an issue for you. Include your relationships with yourself, God, spouses, family, and others.

Table 6-5: Ways Life Would Be Different Without Out-of-Control Behavior

Without behavior 1 my life ________________________________

____

____

____

____

Without behavior 2 my life ________________________________

Without behavior 3 my life

Without behavior 4 my life

Without behavior 5 my life

Without behavior 6 my life

Without behavior 7 my life

Without behavior 8 my life

Without behavior 9 my life

Without behavior 10 my life

Now, doesn't that feel a little better? I hope so. I would encourage you to periodically read what you wrote down here. The road ahead in future chapters might get bumpy for you, so sometimes it's good to remind yourself of where you are going.

My wife, Lisa, and I live in Colorado Springs. We often go for hikes with our children, Hadassah and Jubal. Sometimes these hikes are slightly strenuous. When we remind ourselves of the lake, pond, or view we are headed toward, it makes it easier to endure the journey. You too can benefit by thinking of what your future will be like without these behaviors. So, stick this hopefulness in your backpack and turn the page to discover the second step in our journey.

Chapter Seven

Step 2: Cleansing the Temple

Jed was a very large man from Texas. He came to my office because of several behaviors that were out of control in his life. As we walked through the process described in this book, Jed realized he had a big issue he had to deal with to successfully get a grip on his behaviors. Jed had to face the neglect and abuse he received regularly from his mother. Every time he would visit his mother on holidays he would get all knotted up and would feel full of rage toward his wife and family afterward.

Jed did the cleansing the temple exercise in my office. A short time later, after being home for a few days at Thanksgiving, Jed realized that he didn't have the same knotted-up feelings, nor did he get mad at his wife or family on the way home.

When Nicki came to see me, she was in her twenties and was out of control in an area of her life. She had to face a major betrayal from a boy she had dated in high school. Nicki, who was raised in a Christian home, was the picture of the quintessential popular girl in high school—the beautiful cheerleader dating the football player. But this seemingly ideal situation didn't last long. On a date one night, this boyfriend tried to force himself on her. Nicki ran from the car and called a girlfriend who showed up and gave her a ride home.

When Nicki got to school the next day, she realized that the boyfriend had spread rumors about what had happened, claiming that Nicki had "gone all the way" with him that night. She was humiliated and teased by some of her peers at school. Nicki had to go through the cleansing the temple exercise in my office in order to resolve this traumatic event and help her get a grip on what was controlling her.

I have seen many courageous men and women identify and receive healing from the wounds that others have inflicted on them. All forms of abuse, neglect, infidelity, addictions, and shame can be successfully overcome with the desire to do so.

Regardless of the past, healing can take place. It requires work and patience, but the results are nothing short of marvelous. As a Christian counselor I have witnessed the healing of deep wounds and watched as people have gained victory over controlling behaviors. We serve a great God, and as we co-labor with Him, all things are possible.

The following exercise, called "cleansing the temple," which I also share in my book *Intimacy: A 100-Day Guide to Lasting Relationships,** is designed to help you get a grip on the past hurts and wounds that are at the root of your out-of-control behavior. I have seen tremendous grace come into the hearts of those who follow this exercise.

CLEANSING THE TEMPLE

This exercise can remove a lot of the pain that you may carry in your soul. This pain may be from your city of origin—abandonment, abuse, or improper modeling. It may be from your childhood or past. Some wounds in your soul may even be from your spouse. In some marriages, spouses traumatize one another or deprive one another to such a degree that anger can become an out-of-control behavior displayed in their relationship. Whether anger is the behavior you are dealing

---

* Douglas Weiss, PhD, Intimacy: *A 100-Day Guide to Lasting Relationships* (Lake Mary, FL: Siloam, 2001, 2003).

with or not, if you have wounds that others have inflicted upon your life, follow through with the homework you are about to receive.

The cleansing the temple exercise has its roots in the biblical examples in which Jesus cleansed the temple. The account of this is found in each Gospel. You would do well to take a moment and study each account. The recordings in Scripture of this event are as follows.

> Jesus entered the temple and drove out all who were buying and selling there. He overturned the tables of the money changers and the benches of those selling doves.
>
> —Matthew 21:12

> On reaching Jerusalem, Jesus entered the temple area and began driving out those who were buying and selling there. He overturned the tables of the money changers and the benches of those selling doves.
>
> —Mark 11:15

> Then he entered the temple area and began driving out those who were selling.
>
> —Luke 19:45

> In the temple courts he found men selling cattle, sheep and doves, and others sitting at tables exchanging money. So he made a whip out of cords, and drove all from the temple area, both sheep and cattle; he scattered the coins of the money changers and overturned their tables. To those who sold doves he said, "Get these out of here! How dare you turn my Father's house into a market!"
>
> —John 2:14–16

Each of these accounts contains the principles of the cleansing the temple exercise. First, we will review the four major principles, and then we will walk through the practical application. The following scripture will be our text for this exercise.

> When it was almost time for the Jewish Passover, Jesus went up to Jerusalem. In the temple courts he found men selling cattle, sheep

> and doves, and others sitting at tables exchanging money. So he made a whip out of cords, and drove all from the temple area, both sheep and cattle; he scattered the coins of the money changers and overturned their tables. To those who sold doves he said, "Get these out of here! How dare you turn my Father's house into a market!"
>
> His disciples remembered that it is written: "Zeal for your house will consume me."
>
> Then the Jews demanded of him, "What miraculous sign can you show us to prove your authority to do all this?"
>
> Jesus answered them, "Destroy this temple, and I will raise it again in three days."
>
> The Jews replied, "It has taken forty-six years to build this temple, and you are going to raise it in three days?" But the temple he had spoken of was his body. After he was raised from the dead, his disciples recalled what he had said. Then they believed the Scripture and the words that Jesus had spoken.
>
> —John 2:13–22

BIBLICAL PRINCIPLES

Principle 1: He knew the temple needed to be cleansed.

In most accounts of Jesus cleansing the temple, the temple refers to a physical building in Jerusalem. But in John's account Jesus refers to His body. John 2:18–21 says:

> Then the Jews demanded of him, "What miraculous sign can you show us to prove your authority to do all this?"
>
> Jesus answered them, "Destroy this temple, and I will raise it again in three days."
>
> The Jews replied, "It has taken forty-six years to build this temple, and you are going to raise it in three days?" But the temple he had spoken of was his body.

This is the first insight into the fact that Jesus was changing the dwelling place of God from the physical temple to the temple of a human being. Paul develops this thought a little later when he records that Christian believers are God's temple.

> Don't you know that you yourselves are God's temple and that God's Spirit lives in you? If anyone destroys God's temple, God will destroy him; for God's temple is sacred, and *you* are that temple.
>
> —1 CORINTHIANS 3:16–17, EMPHASIS ADDED

God's plan all along was to dwell inside of us. We are His holy temple. This being true, temples can become defiled through many avenues, including manipulation, abuse, and neglect or abandonment by others. When we become defiled through life, our temple gets defiled also and needs to be cleaned out as well.

It is interesting that Jesus, the owner of the temple, was the one who took full responsibility to clean His own temple. He could have made the money changers and sellers of doves, who were the perpetrators in the story, clean up their own mess, but He didn't. *He* cleansed the temple.

We are the possessors of our temple. If your temple becomes defiled through the abuse of others, you are the one who must clean it up. You are actually the only one who can clean your temple.

Even if it was your spouse who has caused the defilement, he or she cannot clean it out of your temple. Your partner can say he is sorry, but that doesn't get rid of the muck or defilement that has been placed inside your soul.

You must clean up the mess. By cleaning His own temple, Jesus sends a clear message to us: we are responsible to clean our own temples as well.

Principle 2: He identified the sin that caused the defilement.

John's rendition of this Gospel event was as follows: Jesus stated, "Get these out of here! How dare you turn my Father's house into a market!" (John 2:16). Jesus made it very clear to them why He was cleansing the temple. They were taking something holy and misusing it to profit themselves. Most of the people who have hurt you have no concept of your holiness or preciousness. You have felt used or abused during the incidents in which you were wounded. You will need to identify the sin or damage that has been done to you by those who have defiled your temple.

Principle 3: He engaged His anger at the injustice.

Jesus was able to engage His anger at the injustice both verbally and physically. Turning over the tables probably created quite a scene. I am sure that is why the Jews challenged His authority to create such a ruckus.

Jesus wasn't merely having a bad day. This was an act of His will. It was a well thought-out act of obedience. This is an important point to understand, because it will take an act of your will to clean your temple. Once you walk through the rest of the exercises, I believe that it will become an act of obedience as well.

How do I know this was a premeditated act on Jesus' part? Look at John's account of the cleansing of the temple again. "In the temple courts he found men selling cattle, sheep and doves, and others sitting at tables exchanging money. So he made a whip out of cords" (John 2:14–15). This passage gives us the sense that Jesus was looking around and witnessing the peoples' mistreatment of His holy temple. Then, in verse 15, He gathers a bunch of cords, and He takes the time to make a whip, maybe minutes or hours, but He had already decided to use that whip when He entered His temple to cleanse it.

As we proceed with this exercise, you will need to make choices to prioritize your time to prepare for cleansing your temple. Those who have gone about this exercise intentionally and purposefully have received great breakthroughs in their lives.

Principle 4: The temple was restored to its original order.

The story of Jesus cleansing the temple offers a picture of how to heal the wounds inside your temple. After Jesus engaged His righteous rage, His temple was cleansed. Only Jesus had the power to cleanse His own temple. No other prophet or king had done so before Him or after Him. He alone could clean His house. In the same way, we alone can clean our own temples.

I have encountered many wounded souls over the past decade while working with couples and individuals in both inpatient psychiatric hospitals and outpatient office settings. Many of these souls experienced trauma in one form or another, and their wounds were at the very core of their beings.

An individual who has experienced trauma has experienced it in all three levels of his or her being—spirit, soul, and body. All three parts have been defiled, injured, or neglected.

As I train therapists across the country, I stress the three levels at which trauma survivors have been affected—spirit, soul, and body. I ask these individuals, "Why do we just treat trauma cognitively and expect people to heal? If the trauma affects all three dimensions of a person, doesn't it make sense that the healing of trauma involves all three aspects—spirit, soul, and body—as well?" Their heads nod in agreement to this logic.

I share the same logic with you. The concept I am about to suggest to you may seem foreign or uncomfortable at first, but I encourage you to press on. My experience with cleansing the temple has been nothing short of miraculous. Sexual abuse survivors heal very quickly after this exercise. Women who have been sexually betrayed by their husbands move through the stages of grief and forgiveness much more quickly than those who refuse to cleanse their temple.

If your spouse or anyone else has injured you, keep an open mind and try this exercise. Only after you have gone through it will you know whether or not it has been effective.

THE "CLEANSE THE TEMPLE" EXERCISE

1. Write an anger letter.

The first step in the cleansing of your temple is to write an anger letter to the person who has hurt you, but don't send it. Imagine this person in the room with you, but he or she is unable to talk or move. You can say whatever you need to say to him or her in this letter. This is not a letter to suppress your feelings, but rather to vent all the thoughts and feelings of hate, disgust, and anguish that have been robbing your soul. Neither is this an "I forgive you" letter. That will come later. This is the place where you rid yourself of the anger that has been a part of your soul.

2. Get warmed up.

In Jesus' situation, He made a whip for Himself. I don't recommend whips, but a padded baseball bat or tennis racket could be helpful. First, warm up your body. To do this, take your bat and hit a mattress or pillow with small hits. Then use medium, large, and extra large hits. Do this three times. Warm up your voice as well. Shout "No!" each time you hit the pillow. Use small, medium, large, and extra large *nos* with your voice. This may feel awkward, but removing this buildup of pain from your soul and spirit feels almost like having a baby. That is why it's important to be warmed up physically.

While you are warming up, make sure you are home alone. Disconnect the phone so that you are not disturbed.

Note: Consult your doctor if you have a heart condition or other medical problem before attempting this activity.

3. Read your letter aloud.

After your physical warm-up, read aloud the letter you wrote to your offender. If your offender's name is Toby, then you would read as follows: "Toby, how could you have done this to me? I trusted you!"

Of course, Toby is nowhere around. You certainly don't want to do this with him or her around. You are simply in a room alone just reading the letter aloud.

4. Engage your anger physically and verbally.

After reading your letter, pick up your bat. Hit the bed or pillow and symbolically let "Toby" have it. You can yell, scream, or cry, but release the infection that has been robbing you. You can symbolically tell him that his secrets are not controlling you anymore. He was to blame! You have no limits as to what you can say to your offender during this exercise. For once, let go of all of the emotion that is keeping this wound infected. Let it out!

This can last from fifteen minutes to an hour. Your body will let you know when you have completely put this behind you—spiritually, emotionally, and physically.

Someone has given you something toxic, and you have been unhealthy ever since. After you remove it from your spirit, soul, and body, you will be one step closer to getting control over the things that have been controlling you. You're worth getting it all out!

COMMENTS

Work on one offender at a time when doing this exercise. If three different people have offended you, then you will need to complete three different sessions. Do not try to go through this exercise just once for all the different people who have offended you.

If several people have wounded you, make a list of them in the space provided below. Start with the least painful and work your way up to the larger offenses. In this way, you will become more skilled at the exercise and will know what to expect.

You may have different experiences and gain helpful insight as you work through your list. I've known men and women who thought offender number three was the worst, and yet an offender whom they considered less significant actually was a much larger venting experience for them.

Remember, you're cleansing your temple so that as you read through the next several chapters, you can experience freedom from the behaviors that have been controlling you. It's time to use the space below to evaluate yourself.

Table 7-1: Cleansing My Temple

I feel there is some work for me to do to cleanse my temple.

- Yes
- No

The people who have hurt me are:

1. ____________________ 4. ____________________

2. ____________________ 5. ____________________

3. ____________________ 6. ____________________

If you checked *yes* to the above question, take a moment to plan when you can be home alone to do your own cleansing the temple exercise. In the space below, determine the days and times when you can have the house alone. The sooner this takes place, the better. By making a commitment to set aside the time to do this work, you will be much more likely to follow through with it.

Table 7-2: At-Home Schedule for Cleansing the Temple

Monday	a.m.	p.m.
Tuesday	a.m.	p.m.
Wednesday	a.m.	p.m.
Thursday	a.m.	p.m.
Friday	a.m.	p.m.
Saturday	a.m.	p.m.
Sunday	a.m.	p.m.

If you are on the fence as to whether a person needs to be on the list of people who have hurt you, follow this simple rule of thumb. Imagine that the level of emotion in your responses to a person can be categorized in levels from one to ten, with ten being the most severe.

When a person's actions (or your memory of his or her actions) should be responded to with a level two emotional response, and you consistently give responses at an emotional level of seven or eight, you probably have some unresolved anger.

In most cases, if you have any doubt, then it is better to go through the cleansing the temple exercise regarding that person in order to find out for sure if you have unresolved anger. It is far better to discover the truth than to leave emotional blockages inside that can affect your ability to get a grip on the behaviors that have been controlling you. It will be important to complete this exercise before turning the page to learn about the next step in our journey.

CHAPTER EIGHT

Step 3: Forgiving Others and Yourself

Kurt was a man who really needed forgiveness to help him get control over what was controlling him. Kurt was in his thirties, was married to a lovely wife, and was father to three handsome young boys. At one time, Kurt had been a prominent spiritual leader, but he had violated the position by having intimate relationships with more than six women in his congregation.

After his dismissal from the congregation, Kurt went from job to job and became really out of control financially. As Kurt journeyed through the process of getting a grip on what was controlling him (debt), he discovered that he had to forgive someone. That someone was the man he saw every day in the mirror: himself. By following the principles in this chapter, Kurt was able to forgive himself, and he found new freedom as he gained control of his debt and began to heal financially.

Sarah also had to forgive someone before she could get a grip on what was controlling her. You see, Sarah grew up in an alcoholic family. Her father was often drunk and would become violent toward his children and his wife quite frequently. When Sarah was ten years old, her dad, in one of his rages, stormed out the door and never returned. He never called or showed his face to his family again.

Sarah's journey included forgiving her dad not only for the physical and emotional abuse but also for the abandonment. Because of her father's abandonment, she has suffered great fears of her husband leaving her, along with trust issues. Sarah, through the exercises in cleansing the temple and the upcoming forgiveness exercises, was able to unhook herself from her father's abuse and abandonment.

FORGIVING OTHERS

This next stage of healing is only for those who have already cleansed their temple. It should be completed about five days after you have completed the cleansing the temple exercise regarding a particular offender.

Five days or more after finishing your anger work, you should be feeling much better. It is similar to how you feel after getting over a cold. You can feel that the junk in your lungs is gone, and you can breathe clearer and easier now.

The next step to healing is forgiveness, and we will begin by dealing with unforgiveness toward others. I am not suggesting that you look up your violators and tell them you forgive them. Rather, I am talking about doing a therapeutic exercise so that you can see how far along in the process of forgiveness you really are with this person.

The following exercise is very effective, and most are able to choose to forgive their offenders. The Bible is full of teachings on forgiveness. It might be helpful to get a concordance and look up all of the verses listed under the word *forgiveness*. Start with Matthew 6:14–15:

> For if you forgive men when they sin against you, your heavenly Father will also forgive you. But if you do not forgive men their sins, your Father will not forgive your sins.

Work your way through the entire New Testament regarding forgiveness. I realize that for some individuals, healing and cleansing will need to come first before they are truly able to forgive from their heart. For a whole book on the subject of forgiveness, I would recommend the book *The Bait of Satan* by John Bevere.* This book goes into great detail about the importance and value of forgiveness.

This exercise guides you through the process so that you can forgive and have a place in time to mark when your offense was released from your soul. Walk through this exercise with all those on your offender list after you have completed the cleansing exercise for each individual. You will need to be home alone for this exercise, and you will need two kitchen chairs.

THE FORGIVENESS EXERCISE

1. Assume the role of the offender.

Place the two chairs facing each other. Pick a chair, and sit facing the other chair. We'll call the chair in which you are sitting "chair A."

While you are sitting in chair A, role-play your offender. You are now this person. As you role-play this individual, have him or her apologize and ask for forgiveness for all that they have done to you. They are hypothetically confessing to you in the other chair (chair B). If I were doing this exercise about my dad, I would sit in chair A as I role-play my dad. I would verbally own his sin, apologize, and ask for forgiveness for the things I did and didn't do to Doug in chair B.

As I play my dad, I might say, "Doug, I need you to forgive me for..." Now, since I am playing my dad, I can say what he needs to say to me in order to own and apologize for his sin against my life.

2. Role-play your response as the one offended.

Now I have played my dad as he asked forgiveness for several offenses against Doug, who was symbolically sitting in chair B. Yet as the one offended, I heard my dad own his sin and ask forgiveness for it. Now I can start step two.

---

* John Bevere, *The Bait of Satan* (Lake Mary, FL: Charisma House, 1994, 1997, 2004).

I begin by physically moving to sit in chair B, now role-playing myself.

After hearing my dad ask for forgiveness, I now decide how I will respond. Above all, be honest. If you are not ready to forgive your offender, tell him or her.

You could say, "I am just not ready to do this yet, but I will try again in a few weeks."

Whatever you do when you play yourself, don't be a phony or do what you think you *should* do. Do what is real.

If you are able to forgive your offender, then tell him or her. In our example, Doug is now talking to Dad in the opposite chair.

I could say, "Dad, I forgive you."

I could really release him from his abuse and neglect of my soul and the impact his actions had on my life.

If you forgave your offender, move to step three. If at this time you are not able to forgive your offender, get out your calendar and set up a date in about three to four weeks when you will try this exercise again. Do this every month to measure your progress until you are able to forgive.

3. Role-play the offenders' response to forgiveness.

In our example, Doug has forgiven Dad. Now I physically get up, sit down in chair A again, and play the role of my dad. Now it is Dad's turn to respond to Doug's forgiveness.

Dad (role-played by Doug) might say, "Thanks, Doug." When Dad is done talking to Doug the exercise is over.

Let's review:

1. Start in chair A as the offender asking for forgiveness.
2. Now sit in chair B as yourself, and honestly respond to your offender's request for forgiveness.
3. If you have forgiven him or her, go back to chair A and play the offender responding to the forgiveness.

COMMENTS

This can be a very emotional exercise for those with extremely abusive backgrounds, so have a box of tissues nearby. In addition, try to eliminate all possible interruptions—the phone, doorbell, and so forth. It will be important for you to stay focused.

I said this at the beginning of the chapter, but it bears repeating: do this exercise only after you have completed the cleansing the temple exercise. Many individuals attempt to forgive before they heal. Cleansing comes first, then forgiveness.

I will never forget Bryce, a thirty-year-old man whose life savings was taken in a financial scam by an elder in his church. The elder talked Bryce into an investment scam that didn't exist. Bryce had to file bankruptcy, and he lost the respect of his wife and family members.

Bryce went to a counselor who told him to forgive the elder and then he would feel better. He forgave the elder but was having difficulty with anger and depression even three years later. You see, Bryce was told to forgive without first cleansing his temple. After Bryce completed the cleansing the temple exercise regarding the elder, not only was he able to forgive, but he also lost the symptoms that were still there from the trauma of the spiritual and financial betrayal.

Releasing your offenders will free you if you complete your cleansing the temple work first. I have personally experienced much freedom through these exercises given to me by God. I didn't read about these exercises somewhere and Christianize them. They are exercises the Lord gave me in the process of healing myself so that I can heal others also.

In all these exercises, each offender gets his or her time in the chair with you. You must role-play each one and receive an individual apology from each. Don't role-play more than one offender in a day.

FORGIVING YOURSELF

The next step in dealing with this issue of forgiveness is asking forgiveness from yourself. This might sound peculiar, but I have found that if people can own their behavior and forgive themselves for it, they are much more likely to gain control of what has been controlling them. Here is a very practical and successful way of doing this:

Face two chairs toward each other; this is similar to the last exercise when you forgave others. Sit in one chair (chair A) and symbolically imagine yourself in the other chair (chair B). Talk to the self in chair B and ask forgiveness for whatever mistake, choice, or sin you have commited toward yourself. Then move to chair B and respond to yourself (hopefully forgiving yourself). Go back to chair A and respond to being forgiven. Let me give you an example.

In our example, Pat is sitting in chair A. The symbolic "Pat" in chair B will be "Pat 2." An example of Pat's discussion might go something like this:

> PAT: I want you to forgive me for being rebellious as a teen. I used your body to do some drugs. I also had sex with three people before marriage. I lie about you all the time, talking about how good or bad you are. I have never accepted you. I want to ask you to forgive me specifically for my out-of-control behavior of ____________________.
>
> (Pat moves to chair B and now role-plays himself as Pat 2.)
>
> PAT 2: Pat, thank you for being honest. I know you knew about what I've done all along, but it feels good to hear you be so honest. I do choose to forgive you for the many bad choices you made in your youth, for having premarital sex, and for doing drugs. I also forgive you of ____________________.
>
> (Pat moves to chair again and responds to what Pat 2 told him.)
>
> PAT: Thank you so much for forgiving me. I never even thought of asking you to forgive me. I feel better, and I know I can move forward now that you have forgiven me. Thanks again.

This is the kind of experience I have seen often in my office. I strongly encourage anyone with sexual shame to set up two chairs and just do the exercise. Don't spend time evaluating the idea and whether it will work; don't try to process it through until after you have done it. This exercise can really help start flushing out shame issues so that you can be healed and on your way to getting a grip on your behavior.

As you do these exercises and move through forgiveness of others and yourself, you are moving along in your journey toward getting a grip on what has been controlling you. As you do this, the door will swing open to an entirely new and refreshing way of life where you feel free to trust others. This new ability to trust others rather than put up walls of protection is a foundation you will build upon as we head to our next step. If you're ready to move on to our fourth step, turn the page.

Chapter Nine

Step 4: The Power of Disclosure

Welcome to one of the most powerful steps in getting a grip on what's controlling you: disclosure. I can guarantee that by the end of this chapter you will be convinced that disclosure—letting go of secrets—is a powerful life skill to learn.

We will go into discussion on letting go of your secrets, why to tell, and whom to tell. But before we go any further let me introduce you to a few people who have used disclosure to help them gain back control of their lives. The first is Mary.

Mary was your typical housewife. At the time when I met her, she had two adult children and a great husband, Max, who provided well for his family. Mary had always been an avid walker, reader, and very involved in various social events, until she developed a behavior that was controlling her life.

It had started when she was sick with the flu about three years back. Mary lay sick and alone on the sofa because Max was out of town for three days, so she did what any sick American human being would do in the same situation: she turned on her big-screen television!

As she flipped the channels to see what was available, she came upon a shopping network. She paused and became intrigued by the "bargains" being presented. A couple of hours later she grabbed the phone and ordered her first item that day. I say *first* because she picked up the phone and ordered three more times that very same day.

The next day she wasn't feeling much better physically, but she did feel pretty good about the "great deals" she purchased the day before. On the same sofa, watching the same big-screen television, she came upon the shopping channel once again. After she recovered from the flu and Max came back in town, she continued to find herself sitting and waiting for the next great deal on the shopping channel.

Max didn't mind at first because Mary was usually very responsible and thrifty. Eighteen months later, Mary had less social time for others, less time for her children, and was now equipped with her very own credit card to avoid the ever-growing conflicts with Max about her spending.

Mary was ashamed of her behavior and would send many things back after she received them. Mary was experiencing the cycle of out-of-control behavior we discussed in chapter three. She cried, prayed, and even stopped for a few days several times, but she couldn't get a grip on what was controlling her.

Mary's turning point came when she realized that she had incrementally accrued $23,000 of debt. It was then that she knew she had to tell somebody because she was out of control and could no longer keep up the minimum payments on her credit card. She thought and thought. She decided to talk to her pastor of the last fifteen years about her problem.

That day, Mary began a journey toward getting a grip on what was controlling her. She discovered the power of letting go of her secrets.

Tim was a great mechanic who had received promotions every year for the last ten years. He was thirty-two years old and had three young children with his wife, Sandi.

As a boy, Tim had been an only child, and his parents had divorced when he was eight years old. His dad made rare visits for the first few years, but the last time Tim saw him was at the age of twelve.

Growing up, Tim lived close to a Winn-Dixie and frequently stopped by the comic book section of the store to read his favorite comic books. He would spend hours there at Winn-Dixie. Tim would spend any money he had on comic books and eventually started a collection of them. He continued this hobby of reading and collecting comic books into adulthood, and he stored his forty-six boxes of comics at his mom's house.

When he met and married Sandi, she thought this comic book behavior was cute. But when Tim's mother unexpectedly passed away, Tim started to read more and more comic books to cover up his pain. They were under the seat of his truck and in the bathroom and bedroom. Now Tim's spending on comics grew from fifty or sixty dollars a month to two hundred or three hundred dollars monthly. What Sandi thought was cute had now become a wedge between them.

Tim found himself reading comics on the job, during lunch, and before going to bed. One day Tim's friend and boss, Chad, pulled him into the office to discuss Tim's lower performance. This shocked Tim, but it was the turning point he needed to realize that his behavior was out of control. He realized he was stuck but really didn't know what to do.

Sandi suggested that Tim see one of the counselors from the church they attended. He agreed and, as he let go of his secrets, he was able to experience the power of disclosure. This was the beginning of his journey toward getting a grip on what had been controlling him.

WHY SHOULD I TELL?

Right about now you are sitting comfortably in your chair, and a question may be popping into your brain. I can see it coming; as a counselor, I see it regularly. Here's the question: *Why in the world would I tell anyone what is going on with me?*

I know the feeling. I mean, the idea seemed totally preposterous to me as well. I'll never forget how I cried out to God for years to get free from something that was controlling me. Then one day God clearly impressed upon me to tell my roommate about my struggle. I really thought that maybe God was not feeling quite Himself that day! Telling someone that I had a problem seemed like the most insane thing I could do. I remember arguing a little bit about this with God. Thankfully, I finally obeyed His prompting and discovered the power of letting secrets go.

Now let me tell you why the power of letting go of your secrets works to help you begin to get a grip on whatever is controlling you. As a counselor I see so many Christians trapped by out-of-control behavior before they disclose what is controlling them.

For years they cry, pray, repent, and some even fast, but they still are trapped. They cling to 1 John 1:9, "If we confess our sins, he is faithful and just and will forgive us our sins and purify us from all unrighteousness."

This is a great verse, but what this verse promises is that if you confess your sin to God, He will forgive you and cleanse you. This is absolutely true; He will forgive you, and your relationship with Him is cleansed of your sin. This verse absolutely promises forgiveness!

Yet, as wonderful as forgiveness is, if you have developed a behavior that causes you to do the same destructive thing again and again, you need more than forgiveness. You need the power to break the cycle of destruction in your life.

Remember James 5:16 from chapter two? Let's take another look at it.

> Therefore confess your sins to each other and pray for each other so that you may be healed. The prayer of a righteous man is powerful and effective.

This scripture packs a powerful promise! If we actually tell someone (confess our faults), we have the promise that we may be healed. Wow, that's incredible! If we tell another human soul exactly what is going on, we can heal.

Yes, yes, yes, we can heal from what is controlling us! That's the great news of God's Word. The bad news is you and I don't get to choose the method of healing.

Honestly, I didn't like it either. I didn't like the humility that it brought into my life. It is embarrassing to admit failure. Yet, oddly enough, this is the tool that God has chosen to use to heal us.

There is a powerful dynamic that goes on when you disclose and let go of your secrets. It is as if you become more human. Too often we strive to be perfect and cover up the times we fall short of the false self-image we have created. But disclosure allows us to become more humble and teachable, admitting who we truly are to ourselves and to others. When we disclose the darker sides of our humanity, we not only begin to accept ourselves, but we also begin to feel more accepted by others. This is healing in and of itself.

I don't know exactly why God chose the process of letting secrets go as a major part of getting control of what is controlling you, but I have a theory. I believe God has one major objective in our lives: to make us more Christlike.

The purpose of our relationship experiences—whether good or less than good—is to make us more like Christ. Therefore, it is absolutely ingenious of God to make us go through a process that grants us humility (whether we like it or not) in order to free us from the behaviors that control us.

All of us battle with pride in varying degrees, but it is important to realize that the enemy uses pride to keep us under the control of sinful behavior in our lives. When we are too proud to disclose our imperfections and darkness, we stay trapped in our own prison.

The key that frees us out of our self-made prisons is disclosure. When we insert disclosure into the lock, it opens, and we can walk in our newfound humility and freedom.

I know that, at first, disclosure can sound scary and intimidating. It did to me! But now I find it easy to disclose, because I know that it is the powerful path to even more freedom in my life. The more I disclose, the freer I become.

Just last night I had to practice disclosure with my wife over a somewhat humorous incident. It wasn't even dark or sinful, but closer to what you would describe as a "gray area." Yet I disclosed it to her immediately because I don't want any secrets in my life. I don't want to give the enemy any openings to come in and start his pattern of destruction. My wife and I laughed afterward, and, most importantly, I was forgiven and felt free once again.

So why does disclosure work? The Scripture states that if we bring something to the light, it becomes light. (See Ephesians 5:13.) Can you remember being afraid of something in the corner of your bedroom at night as a child? There you were, probably covering your head with the blanket, convinced that a monster lurked at the foot of the bed, only to find that it was just a simple toy or article of clothing when the light was turned on.

The same is true of our sin. When we keep it hidden in the dark, the enemy can play all sorts of mind games with us, and the problem can seem overwhelming, paralyzing us with fear. But when our situation is brought into the light, we can look at it for what it is and deal with it honestly. This new perspective brings renewed strength and sweet relief to our lives.

I also want to share with you a theological principle that my clients have found very helpful. I'll try to be brief in explanation.

Get out your Bible, open it to the Gospels, and read every account of Jesus appearing to people after His death and resurrection. Notice anything missing? If you don't have your Bible handy, I'll help you out. Jesus appeared to two men on the road to Damascus, to Mary Magdalene, to ten of His disciples, and then to eleven of them (Thomas included). Finally He appeared to five hundred people.

Any guess as to what is missing in each of these occurrences? Jesus most likely had an opportunity to heal, yet there is no record of Him healing anyone after His resurrection.

Now turn to the next book after the Gospels: the Book of Acts. In the Book of Acts we see the apostles healing people all over the place. Before Jesus had returned to heaven, He had promised to send the Holy Spirit. When the Spirit filled Christ's followers on the Day of Pentecost, the healing power of Jesus began flowing through the body of Christ (Christians).

This shows us we can go to members of Christ's body, the church, when we need healing. The next time you are in church, look around. In those earthen vessels is the power of God to help you heal from whatever is controlling you.

To drive this point home when I'm speaking at conferences, I often have people face each other and look at each other as the path to healing. It's an amazing moment as hearts really see the power of letting secrets go as a path to healing.

This reality should fill you with hope. Your Christian brothers and sisters can be instruments of God's healing power in your life, bringing freedom over the behaviors that have been controlling you. Now, as you consistently disclose and let your secrets go, you can expect healing to begin.

WHOM SHOULD I TELL?

This is usually the next question that percolates in an intelligent mind. Once you realize that you have to tell someone, you immediately want to evaluate the type of person with whom you should share your less-than-wonderful parts. There are many characteristics to look for when choosing what I call a *primary person*—a person to whom you are going to disclose your secrets.

Don't fall into the trap where some people get caught: they give all their effort evaluating people, looking for perfect people and never finding them. The result is that they never get a grip on whatever is controlling their lives because they rule out everyone else as untrustworthy. I call these people *personal evaluators.*

Personal evaluators will peer out of their souls' windows at the flaws in everyone else. In their minds this justifies why they shouldn't be honest with others. Let me remind you that James 5:16 does *not* say "confess your faults to perfect people." The author didn't qualify the other person in any way except they also were human and had Christ in them.

So, if you are a personal evaluator, you will find that there are no perfect people to choose from. All people are flawed. It may or may not occur to you that you are also flawed. Worse yet, you need these imperfect, flawed people to help you if you want to get a grip on whatever is controlling you.

So, exactly what do you need to look for in a person to whom you confide? I've narrowed the list to the following seven characteristics.

1. Someone who is honest

A valuable characteristic of someone to confide in—especially when confessing an area that has control of you—is honesty. Why did I choose honesty first?

It is my personal and clinical opinion that honest people seem to have already looked at their own flaws. Honest people have minimal denial about who they are because they have learned to accept themselves. If they can accept themselves, they will be more likely to accept you, even the flawed you.

Honest people, in my experience, are able to see "both sides" of people and situations as opposed to those who think in "either/or" categories. For example, they can hear you discuss the food, work, sex, entertainment, hobbies, or other things that are controlling you *and* be able to see the many good things in you as well.

Lisa, my wife, is an honest person. She can see both flaws and strengths in a person. If we are discussing flaws in someone, she is quick to see strengths in them as well. So I encourage you to involve an honest person in this step of your recovery from out-of-control behavior.

2. Someone who can keep a confidence

This is a critical characteristic that anyone with whom you are going to share your "buried treasure" needs to possess. By *buried treasure,* I mean the things that may be controlling you and the other stuff that is buried in your soul.

Nobody likes to be betrayed, especially when being vulnerable. Many of us know what it feels like to disclose something that makes you vulnerable and then have it come up in future conversations, assaults, or jokes.

I have been around a lot of Christian people throughout the years. One of the things I evaluate about people I choose to be in relationship with is how they talk about other people. I can tell a lot about people by what flows out of their mouths after I bring up a mutual acquaintance. I will often start a conversation by saying, "I believe you know John or Jane Doe?"

If they automatically bring up the best about John or Jane and continue on that tract, generally, I learn that they can keep confidences. If, however, they start telling me their "concerns" about John or Jane, I will have concerns about their ability to keep confidences. If they really start uncovering or exposing John or Jane, I feel very unsafe around them. I know that they will also share their observations about my flaws with someone else pretty readily.

Listen to the Spirit of God, and follow your intuition about choosing your primary person. Be sure that they can keep confidences. I have a friend, Bill, to whom I can tell anything. I love and value the safety of a friend who can keep confidences.

3. Someone who is available

When you involve someone as your primary person, it is very important that they are available to you. By *available,* I mean that a person is able to take your call in a moment of need. He or she will also have spiritual wisdom and a willingness to pray with you at your request.

Keep in mind that physical distance can be a factor in considering how available someone is. If a person is the most godly, wonderful person you know, but he or she lives in another state or country, his or her availability will be much more limited than someone who lives across town.

You should also realize that availability has to do with more than physical distance. If a person is in the middle of a personal or family crisis, he or she may not be as available to you. You will need someone available to hear you as you start to get a grip on what is controlling you.

Last but not least, you will also want to respect this individual's life and family. If you've ever seen the movie *What About Bob?* you'll know what I mean! When you find a person who can be available to you, ask about the best location (home, office, on the road) as well as best times to call; then respect those boundaries. When you call, get to your point quickly so you both can continue on with your previously planned days. Your primary person is going to try to help support you; therefore, you will want to try to respect his or her life and family in the process as well.

4. Someone who is accepting

Another characteristic to look for in a primary person is acceptance of others. An accepting person is not judgmental. We all know the type: rigid Christians who judge everyone but themselves. This is the last thing you need as you open up to someone.

There is a great difference between the *religious* heart and the *spiritual* heart. The religious heart is fluent in the language of "judgmental-ese" and will often say things such as, "You should," "You should have known better," and "I told you so." This type of Christian tends to build *walls* rather than *bridges* between people.

Accepting people are generally more fun to be with on any journey. They can laugh freely at life, at jokes, and even at themselves.

I travel regularly, and I would much rather be accompanied by an authentic, accepting person rather than someone who is trying to live up to an image.

The person trying to portray an image has difficulty with other people being authentic or flawed and rarely will let someone get close enough to really feel connected. If you try to disclose your secrets to this type of person, you are more likely to feel patronized than accepted.

One of the ways I evaluate if someone is accepting is to listen to how they talk about people's mistakes, including their own. If they are able to own their mistakes and easily apologize to others, this is a sign that they will be accepting of flaws and mistakes in others.

On the flip side of this, if they are able to easily forgive others, this shows that they are accepting, but if I am still hearing about a mistake from months ago that someone already owned and apologized for, this person's heart may be more judgmental than accepting. As you get a grip on what is controlling you I recommend that you recruit an accepting person to be on your side. It will make letting go of your secrets a safer and more pleasant experience.

5. Someone who is not family

When you are going through the process of letting go of secrets, it is best if family is not your main support. Family is family. They may or may not be able to keep confidences. Family is for life. What seems smooth sailing now may be stormy when one of you makes different choices with your lives.

Even in the best of families I strongly recommend when you are thinking of sharing what is controlling you that you go outside of the family. They can be a great support and may even have an idea of what is going on, but it's best that you do not engage a family member as the person to whom you will disclose your secrets.

As a counselor, I have sat in many groups and have been the primary person for both clients and friends. I find that people are much more likely to be totally honest with friends than they are with family.

A friend is also better than family if you need to be confronted. (I like to call it being "care-fronted.") People will generally take this type of loving confrontation better from a friend than a family member. If a family member gave you the same correction, you might not be able to hear it with as much clarity as you would from a friend.

So, for your sake and your family's sake, please choose a friend to be your primary person. If you want to let family know what has been going on, use your judgment, but keep them in a support role so they can still be your family.

6. Someone who is spiritually mature

The issue of spiritual maturity is a great characteristic for someone to whom you are going to open up. Now don't go looking for "Jesus with skin on." Even the most spiritually mature person has quirks, flaws, and some less-than-great ideas.

Instead, look for someone who regularly seeks God and allows God into his or her life to improve it. Does this person regularly reference his or her walk with God throughout regular conversation? Does the way this person communicates change when he or she is not around church people? If he passes this litmus test for spiritual maturity and stability, you can probably take a risk.

As you share your heart, even those things that are confusing you, a spiritual person will meet this with compassion. As you begin to grow, the spiritual person will most often feed you encouragement. The fruit of encouragement nourishes your soul to walk in the grace that God has given you.

A really neat thing about having spiritually mature people in your life is that they can pray with you. Now, I don't know about you, but I love when people can really pray with me. I mean, they can reach God and connect Him to where I am. They are comfortable connecting with God and with others. Spiritually mature people are great to have alongside you as you begin to take back the control over what is controlling you.

7. Someone professional

I know that some of you still have real trust issues, and for you, opening up is a real step of faith. Well, that doesn't mean you are allowed to avoid this principle in your healing. If you have issues with trusting people, the first step might be to go to a professional such as a pastor, priest, spiritual leader, or counselor as your primary person. Why? Because many of them adhere to a professional code of ethics that prohibits them from sharing what you have to say with others. In the case of a licensed counselor, it would be illegal for them to discuss your issues with anyone else without your permission.

For some, this extra safety net is helpful to overcome their fear of trust and start opening up. Another great benefit of starting with a professional is that many of them are educated, trained, and have years of experience with the human condition of being "flawed but loved." They don't expect people to be wonderful all the time in every area of their lives. They know you can have secrets, and they are not afraid of your secrets. You will probably not shock them. I personally like it when I have a problem—whether it is a personal problem, financial problem, etc.—and the person I'm talking to has not only heard it before but also has a great possibility of actually helping me.

Many pastors, priests, and spiritual leaders have some training in counseling, which may be really helpful to you as you open up. A trained counselor has spent anywhere from four to ten years training themselves in the spiritual, psychological, and biological issues that can impact you and impede your ability to get a grip on what is controlling you.

I see this great sense of relief in my office every day. A man is trapped by something that is controlling his life. For the first time he opens up about his issue. After the initial feeling of letting the proverbial cat out of the bag, we start talking about the issue and making strategies for getting a grip on what's controlling him. Then it is as if his soul has a huge sigh of relief. It is as if his eyes say, "You understand; you accept me and think I can actually get a grip on this." My eyes beam with optimism because it is "not my first rodeo," and I know with some work and some checkpoints built into the process he can be victorious—the way his heart wants to be and knows he can be.

A licensed counselor does cost money, but it really is worth it. I have ten counselors who work alongside of me at my counseling center in Colorado Springs. The wisdom that God has given them through His Word, His Spirit, their training, lives, and professional experiences is absolutely worth their hourly rate. So if you need that extra safety net, I would say go for it! You are worth whatever it takes or costs to get a grip on what is controlling you.

THE WHOLE ENCHILADA!

OK, here is where we get really radical. There's an expression that says, "You are as sick as the secrets you keep." Although most of us know we are as sick as our secrets, many of us still keep them! I cannot tell you the hundreds and hundreds of people who have told me, "You're the first person I have ever told this to!" Although I think it's great that they have finally decided to break open, I also feel sad that they have waited so long.

I know that a little seed of a secret brings forth a whole tree of shame and/or guilt. You carry this heavy weight in your soul that often keeps you unable to get a grip on your life. You see, in my career as a counselor I have seen a direct connection between secrecy and self-destructive behavior.

Conversely I have also seen the power of letting go of secrets and bringing them into the light, not just to God but to another person. This is where the concept of the whole enchilada comes in. Most people tend to open up about one secret at a time. But this can take years or decades. The better way to approach disclosure is to share all of your secrets at one time.

Let me tell you a true story. Ellen and Erik had been married for over twenty years. They looked like the perfect Christian couple. On the outside they were attractive, smart, and successful. Their children were highly active in church and respected for their character.

But Ellen and Erik had a big secret. They hadn't been sexual in years. Nobody knew this secret about their intimate life. This nonsexual marriage was controlling both of their lives, and it looked like a divorce was imminent.

Ellen felt there were secrets that Erik had not been telling her. When they came into my counseling center, we talked about their lack of trust and Ellen's concern about secrets. Ellen wanted Erik to take a polygraph exam to continue in the marriage. Erik did not want to do this, which made Ellen even more suspicious that there were secrets, and she was furious.

It was obvious that Erik was being unfaithful to his wife. He finally broke down and told Ellen about his secret life of porn and prostitutes that had been going on throughout their marriage. All of the secrets were out within one hour. The polygraph verified Erik's new honesty with Ellen. After three days of intensive couples therapy, they were well on their way to healing and restoring the intimacy of their marriage together.

I remember receiving information early in my Christian walk about being totally honest with another person about everything. I thought about it, and like most Christians who are asked to be totally honest, put it off indefinitely. After all, I was forgiven, right?

It is true that I was forgiven and Jesus loved me, but time and time again the Holy Spirit would bring this principle of sharing "the whole enchilada" of my past with another person. So, eventually, it became a point of obedience for me.

I honestly didn't understand the value of telling the whole enchilada of my exact sins to another person, but I just knew I had to do it. Once I knew with whom I was to share all my secrets, I wrote down all of the garbage inside of me. I made a list of what I had done and to whom I had done it. Let me tell you, that was not fun at all.

Then I got together with the person with whom I was going to share my whole enchilada of sin. I went through it detail by detail. He listened, forgave me, and I felt obedient. But that's not the end of the story.

Within minutes, I felt the cleansing presence of the Holy Spirit. It was like lightning hitting my body. I was free, totally free. All of my past feelings of "If you knew me, you wouldn't love me" were powerfully removed. I was washed. I was so fired up by my newfound sense of freedom over my past that I went to a football stadium and danced in the middle of the field in broad daylight, thanking God for my healing.

Ever since, I have felt free to shamelessly worship God and to look others in the eye and be totally "seen" by them. Few things in the process of my healing have had greater lifelong impact than sharing the whole enchilada. Letting loose of all my secrets was definitely a milestone in getting a grip on what had control over me. Although it has been many years since that event, I can tell you where I was sitting, with whom, and even what time it was.

If the Holy Spirit prompts you to share the whole enchilada as part of getting a grip on what is controlling you, do it as soon as possible. I know you might be having all kinds of feelings right about now. Shame from one secret can keep a soul stuck in self-destructive behaviors for a lifetime. But please believe me when I tell you that the freedom you will experience is worth overcoming your fear of sharing the whole enchilada. Living the life you were meant to live is worth it; helping others find the same freedom you are about to find is worth it. I don't believe God would be using me as much as He has, had I not told the whole enchilada.

Letting loose of your secrets is the fourth step in our journey from pride and self-protection to humility and vulnerability. Don't just think or feel about whether to do it or not; ask God. That's right; just close this book and ask God about the information we covered in letting loose of all your secrets. Ask what you are to do and with whom. He will answer, and when He does, you will have the confidence to do what He says, because He knows what you need.

Disclosure is a huge step in getting control of your behavior. But it is not the last step. You still have more excitement ahead of you! So pick up your foot and climb up to step five with a lighter heart.

CHAPTER TEN

Step 5: Exercise Positive Behavior

Many of you have areas that have controlled your life for years, even decades. You may have made efforts here and there with various degrees of success. In this chapter, I will outline five positive behaviors for you to begin to exercise in your life as the next step in gaining control over your behavior.

CONTROLLING YOUR BEHAVIOR VS. CONTROLLING YOUR EMOTIONS

As we embark on this portion of our journey together, I must warn you that I am not instructing you to control your *emotions*. I am giving you principles that will help you control your *behavior*. It is important to realize the difference. Here are three examples to help you understand the difference between a behavior-based approach to getting a grip and an emotion-based approach.

Matt was controlled by his anger and believed it was just out-of-control emotions. When he was able to see that it was out-of-control behavior, he was able to start making progress. Matt could not figure out how to get a grip on an emotion, but he was able to get a grip on his angry behavior.

Luci was controlled by overeating for twenty-five years. She had some pain in her soul to address, as many of us do. After dealing with her emotional pain, the drive to overeat became reduced, but she still was controlled by food. When Luci shifted her perspective and saw eating as a behavior, she started to make progress. She was then able to move forward and get a grip on her eating habits.

Erica, a twenty-six-year-old business school student, had the exact opposite problem as Luci. She was controlled by an eating disorder. She was obsessed with body fat. She was grossly underweight and needed to break this cycle of unhealthy behavior. She not only had to address her "city of origin" issues, but she also had to begin new behaviors to reinforce a healthy eating pattern in her life.

Are you starting to see the difference? Lasting change requires a *paradigm shift,* a change in your former way of thinking about your out-of-control behavior. You have to stop thinking of what's controlling you as an emotion and start thinking of it as a behavior. Moving from an emotion-based life to a behavior-based life is a major factor in getting a grip on what is controlling your life, and the best way to get started with a focus on behavior is to start exercising your "positive behavior muscles."

FIVE WAYS TO EXERCISE YOUR "POSITIVE BEHAVIOR MUSCLES"

These five exercises outline new behaviors that you can practice daily or regularly to start getting a grip on what is controlling you. As you practice these behaviors, you will learn a very important life skill. You will learn to do the right thing regardless of how you feel. As you consistently practice these behaviors, you will begin to master *your will* to move in a positive direction.

1. Pray

As you read these pages, you might be saying to youself, *Why is prayer first?* Well, it is important to have God's help when you are trying to get a grip on what has been controlling you. After all, you may have tried by yourself many times. You need God when you run out of ideas, strength, or resolve to see something through.

I know from experience as a counselor that few Christians really pray. I remember speaking to a large group of churchgoing parents about sexual issues related to raising teens. I asked the crowd how many of them prayed for their teenagers daily or regularly. Notice I didn't say pray *with* your teen but *for* them. Significantly less than half of these very sincere Christian parents were not engaging prayer in their raising of their teenagers.

I have also counseled many Christian couples for marital issues. In most cases these couples are not praying with each other, and haven't for years or decades.

Remember what the Bible says about us building a house? Psalm 127:1 states, "Unless the LORD builds the house, its builders labor in vain." If we are going to "build a house," so to speak, to get a grip on what is controlling our lives, we need God first in the process.

I wouldn't dream of attempting marriage or parenting without prayer. I also wouldn't dream of battling for control of an area of my life—be it weight, finances, friendships, business, attitudes, or other issues—without prayer.

Prayer works for many reasons. First, it puts us in regular relationship with the God of heaven and earth. He is a great God as well as a great person. He has a heart and wants to be related to—not just talked at, the way some of us do in prayer. Prayer is sharing and listening. It is communication between friends. Jesus said in John 21:5 that He calls us friends.

I enjoy a good exchange with my friends. When we get together, we share with each other and listen to each other. In the same way, prayer is the friendship exchange between God and His children.

Second, prayer allows us to humble ourselves and become willing to receive ideas from God that can really help us. Although our problems might seem huge to us, He is able to hear and help as we walk through a process such as this.

Here's a story from my own life to help illustrate what I mean. When I was just starting college, my mind wasn't the sharpest due to things that had been controlling my life prior to Jesus becoming my Lord and Savior. About that time, I read an article on Lethician and how it helps improve memory. I made it a matter of prayer, and I felt prompted by the Holy Spirit to purchase some and try it out.

Since taking it, my memory has improved tremendously. Because of this, I have rarely missed a day of taking Lethician for the last twenty years. You see, because I brought this before the Lord as a matter of prayer, my heart was open to the answer He gave me. God directed me to an unexpected source that helped me to get a grip on the lingering effects of an out-of-control area of my life.

Third, prayer is powerful. As you take the journey to get a grip on your life, it will be critical to spend time in focused, daily prayer concerning what is controlling your life. In Luke 18, we find a story of a widow who would regularly pursue a judge for justice. She received what she asked for because of her persistence. Consistent and persistent daily prayers bring powerful results.

So whether it be anger, fear, food, lust, entertainment, sports, people, money, or any other issue, make it a point to pray daily about the area that is out of control in your life. You deserve to have control over what is controlling your life. Prayer is the first positive behavior to reaching this goal.

2. Read

Oh my, Dr. Doug, you don't really mean crack a book, do you? Actually, yes! Really! I want you to crack every book you can find on the behavior you are aiming to overcome.

I have worked with many people who suffered from a variety of things that had control of their lives. I am always surprised when clients come to my office for help with issues such as sexual addiction, and they haven't read one book on the subject. When you are dealing with a particular issue, reading is critical in order to find the right "tools for your toolbox."

You might be saying, "But I don't like to read!" Try purchasing an audio version of your book on CD or cassette tape. Reading, listening to tapes, and so forth are ways to directly gain more information and ideas that can help you. Go to the library, Amazon.com, or Christian

Web sites; buy several books on the subject, and start reading daily. Plan to spend about ten to fifteen minutes a day reading. In addition to providing you with helpful information, this exercise will keep you vigilant about getting a grip on your life.

You will pick up some ideas along the way as you read these books. Every tip and insight can be a valuable tool. One seemingly small idea can spark something that motivates you or breaks you out of your cycle, moving you closer to regaining control.

Still not convinced? Take a moment and think about who usually writes these types of books. The authors are typically experts in their field with doctorates in their area of expertise. These authors can also be heroes who have overcome and learned a lot of the answers the hard way. Through books or tapes, you can lock these experts in a room, so to speak, and absorb some pretty amazing information for a fraction of what it would cost to spend even an hour with a professional counselor.

Another advantage of having your library well stocked is that God will start sending people to you because you have the information to help. The Bible tells us that in our weakness, He is made strong. I have run across so many people whose mess became their message. Who knows? Maybe you will write one of these books in the future.

So read, read, read. Study your area of weakness, and take this positive behavior to heart.

3. Group meetings

One time I heard a speaker in our church tell a story about a couple who lived on a farm in the country. This couple was faithful to their little church for decades. They raised their children there and gave their lives into this little country church. One Sunday the husband said, “I’m not going to church anymore!” His wife went on to church without him that day and told the pastor what her husband had said.

The wise old pastor came to visit the farmer on a cold winter day. The pastor knocked at the farmer's door, and the farmer invited him in. The two men naturally headed to two chairs facing the fire where they spent many visits over the years.

As they sat and quietly watched the fire blaze, the pastor got out of the chair and pulled a piece of burning wood out of the fire and placed it just slightly away from the rest of the burning logs.

Time went on, and the two men continued to sit quietly in their chairs. After a while, the wood that the pastor had removed from the fire became cool. Eventually, it went completely cold while the rest of the fire burned on and on.

The wise pastor rose from his chair and walked to the door. The farmer let the pastor out and said, "I'll be there Sunday."

The farmer got the pastor's message: when we huddle up we do better.

Unfortunately, many of us—especially Americans—act as if independence is the ultimate stage of human growth and development. Actually, independence is only the second stage of growth. In the first stage, you are dependent on your parents. They change your diapers and give you food and clothes. As you grow, you become more and more independent from your parents. By the time you reach adulthood, they no longer need to pay anything for you or take care of you.

At this point you actually are independent. But this is not the final stage of growth. Even though you no longer *need* your parents, you can *choose* them. Then you become interdependent. You both choose each other, not out of need but out of a desire to be in a relationship. *Interdependence* is the third and final stage of growth, not *independence.* Choosing others is critical to get—and keep—a grip on what is controlling you.

Small group meetings have been a mainstay of Christianity, and they are definitely experiencing resurgence. I thank God for the recovery movement and small group leaders in churches everywhere who are addressing issues such as addiction, abuse, divorce, and many others.

By telling you to attend group meetings, I am recommending that you commit yourself to a group process, preferably in your local area. However, teleconference or Internet support groups work as well.

The principle here is community. You build a community of people around you who are committed to getting a grip on the same area of life as you. A successful example of this would be Weight Watchers. People who are trying to lose weight by participating in Weight Watchers regularly meet in groups and report both their progress and their setbacks.

In a healthy group process, members work together as a team. Sometimes in a group, your denial about what you are doing in your life is revealed, and for the first time, you can clearly see your behavior and its effects on your life and the lives of those around you. You then receive affirmation for your effort to get a grip on your behavior, and you are held accountable for the times when you slip up. Also I find that people who utilize a group stay motivated and focused on their goals.

Another great aspect of being part of a small group focused on your area of need is that you benefit from giving support to others. I often find that when I give to others I also receive. As you support each other on your journey to gain control over what's been controlling you, everybody grows.

Imagine if you were in a group of people who were committed to getting a grip on what was controlling them. Each person was just doing the three positive behaviors we have covered so far. Each prayed daily asking God for help and ideas. Each was reading the best authors and giving great ideas on the same issue. Each had motivation and degrees of success. I'm excited even writing about this.

I think you get the point. You would be surrounded by like-minded and like-hearted people. You would have to try really hard to fail in this environment. This is an environment full of opportunity to grow.

Meeting with a group is a critical part of the process of getting a grip on what is controlling you. Look at your attempts in the past; did they involve a group meeting? If not, did you try by yourself to be successful and fail? I suggest you try meeting with a small group to regain control of this controlling behavior.

Usually in larger communities there are plenty of groups to support you, but it may take some research to find a group. After research, if you can't locate a group, start one yourself.

Most churches are fertile ground for starting such groups. I have even known people who simply posted the start of a group in the calendar section of their local newspaper and started a successful group that way. Be resourceful and determined in forming your group—even if it is just a couple of friends who love you enough to get together with you on a weekly basis.

You deserve the power of a small group in your life as you move toward getting a grip on what is controlling you. This is a gift you give to yourself to shore up your potential to be successful this time.

4. Daily calls

The fourth positive behavior is to commit to daily phone calls to either other group members or a primary person. The calls keep you very focused on your goals for getting a grip on what is controlling you.

No matter what type of behavior has control over you, check in with someone daily for at least the first one hundred days. You can check in on how you are doing with your five positive behaviors. You can share what you are reading, how prayer is working, and how your group meetings are going.

The energy that you put into calling this person works its way into a regular discipline that begins to drown out the voices of fear, anger, compulsive behaviors, and other behaviors that might be plaguing you.

As you continue to make success, you will look forward to the encouragement of your daily phone call. On the days you are struggling, that phone call can help you through a rough spot. I know many clients who have told me just the fact that they knew they would be talking to someone about their behavior helped them get through a particular situation without reverting to their old pattern of out-of-control behavior.

Countless numbers of clients tell me that when they were feeling like reverting to their out-of-control behavior they made their daily call instead. The calm person on the other end was able to encourage them, comfort them, pray for them, and at times even just laugh with them.

Having someone give you an immediate reality check or a different way to see things is paramount as you walk through the process of getting a grip on what is controlling you. Also, it is great to receive phone calls from others in your group. It is amazing how God can use you to speak to someone else and encourage you at the same time. I cannot even count the times I have gotten off the phone with someone and thought, *I needed to hear what I just said to the other person who called me for help.* The journey of getting a grip on what is controlling you is a team effort. Phone calls make this a very supportive adventure.

Unfortunately, I have also heard from people who did not utilize positive behavior number four and relapsed into their problematic behavior as a result. I don't know what it is that makes us humans want to do everything without help. We actually need each other. Reaching out daily in humility to acknowledge that you need someone else will have a direct impact on your success in getting a grip.

As a counselor, I have found that phone calls have a direct correlation to success. When someone comes into my office and tells me they have relapsed on a particular behavior they have been targeting,

I immediately ask how they are doing with their phone calls. Almost always the phone calls started to slack for a few days or weeks before they began to relapse into their old pattern of behaviors.

I remember one client that went through several relapses before he was able to accept the simple science he was proving: when he called, he stayed in control of his behavior, and when he didn't, he lost control of his behavior. Once he accepted his own scientific experience, he was able to remain in control of his particular behavior.

So in the first one hundred days, I strongly encourage you to call, call, call. Remember, the calls are not just for you; they can make someone else's day as well.

*5. **Pray again***

Yes, we start with prayer and end with prayer. Somewhere at the end of your day, thank God for your newfound freedom from what has been controlling you all these years. Even one day of freedom is better than one more day stuck with the behaviors that have been controlling your life.

Thank God for His help today. He might have helped you in a situation or even kept you from one you did not know about. He might have quickened you to remember your goals, a Bible verse, or just prompted you to call someone. Without God's help you might have stayed the same today, and for most, that would be a pity.

One of the things I have learned about God's personality is He likes to be thanked. Actually, I think He loves grateful children the same way we do. It blesses a parent's heart when a child says, "Thank you," or "I love you," and leaves little notes that are barely legible and presents that are barely identifiable.

There is a counselor in my office who is always grateful. He buys presents, takes people to lunch, and is truly pure-hearted in his gratefulness. He is someone everyone loves to be around. I think God enjoys being around grateful children as well.

It is good for us to be in a position of gratefulness. God is worthy of praise just because of who He is.

That's why part of getting a grip is just connecting with God at the end of the day. Prayer slows you down long enough to hear from God, too. Remember, prayer is a two-way dialogue. At the end of the day if God chooses to share with you, that can be an amazing thing.

So, settle down somewhere quiet and listen to God. That's good advice for everyone, but it is imperative for those who are trying to get a grip on controlling behaviors.

As you implement the five exercises of praying, reading, group meetings, daily calling, and prayer again, you can see your positive behaviors developing. You are growing spiritually, relationally, and cognitively, and gaining victory over the behavior that has been controlling you all these years.

There is something else that is growing while you exercise these five positive behaviors, and it is your will. Your will is being exercised to do what you are committed to instead of doing what you feel like. As your will gets stronger, it can help control the behavior you are currently trying to get a grip on.

The will it takes to pray, go to a meeting, read, or call others is the same will it will take to set anger, fear, lust, greed, envy, or other out-of-control behavior in place. My pastor, Ted Haggard, has a saying: "The same willpower it takes to say no to a Twinkie when you are fasting is the same willpower it takes to say no to other sins."

The great thing about these five behaviors is that, in doing them, you are exercising your willpower and you don't even know it. It reminds me of a friend of mine in college who was learning to tread water but hated practicing in the pool. I wanted to help him out, so I jumped in a pool with him and agreed I would get out when he got tired. We got into a great conversation, and a whole hour went by. Suddenly we realized that he had been treading water that entire time, but he didn't know it.

As you put these five positive behaviors into action, you are like my college friend. You are exercising your "good behavior muscles" without even knowing it. As you push past your emotions every day, you will find you are more able to choose the positive behavior than the one that is currently controlling you.

Chapter Eleven

Step 6: Measure Me, Please

Now we come to a critical fork in the road. I begin this chapter with a warning to you: as you read through the next several pages, you might get angry, indignant, or even want to stop. We're going to talk about being measured, and it can be a real challenge for some people. If those feelings come up, I encourage you to keep turning the pages! Let me get started with a few examples from my counseling experiences.

John was a deacon in his church. He was a pilot for mostly domestic flights, traveling three to four days a week. His wife, Karen, was a wonderful woman, raising two girls, singing in the choir, and going to soccer practices several times a week.

John had a secret life on the road that carried over from his military days. When he was on the road, he would drink alcohol, go to strip clubs, and watch pornography. This had gone on for twelve of the sixteen years of John and Karen's marriage.

One day John came home, and he looked awful. He was incredibly quiet that night, and finally, after the girls were in bed, he told Karen he had to talk to her. She thought maybe he was being laid off from work or he had an accident. She was not prepared for the words that would slowly come out of John's mouth. "I have gonorrhea, and you probably do as well." Immediately Karen began to convulse, cry, and scream as John confessed a one-time incident of unfaithfulness.

Months went by, and Karen was not handling it any better. Her spirit was telling her she did not know the truth, even though John swore he had told her everything. Things got really bad, and they talked to their pastor, who referred them to my office.

They began to tell their story, and sure enough, Karen started to cry, convulse, and scream again. She had lost fifteen pounds since John confessed, and she was tiny already to start. The wear and tear of this pain was obvious on Karen's face.

I asked John, "If you could do anything to help Karen get rid of this pain, would you do it?"

"Yes," he said.

"Anything?"

"Yes, Dr. Doug. I love my wife."

I said, "OK, then let me call our polygraph examiner. You can take a polygraph and give your wife the gift of knowing she knows the truth. Once she knows that she has the whole truth she can begin to heal."

You should have seen John's face. All the blood left his face, and he became extremely quiet. Karen began to ask him if there was more than one. As the story unraveled, John revealed that he had been sexually involved with more than twenty-five people, had regularly visited strip clubs, and had engaged in drinking and soliciting prostitutes.

As he told the truth, amazingly Karen stayed calm. He did take the test and proved he was now telling the truth. It was the reality of being measured that caused John to tell the truth, and he and Karen could now begin to heal.

Now, I'm not recommending the polygraph for you, don't worry! What I am moving toward is the idea of measuring yourself so you can be truthful about your situation and begin to heal.

Lane and Jenny were clients who were trying to complete the intimacy exercises in my book *Intimacy: A 100-Day Guide to Lasting Relationships.* The book encourages couples to do three exercises daily. Well, Lane and Jenny were having a telephone counseling session with me one day, and they spent quite a bit of time disagreeing over how much they did the three daily exercises. I asked them to keep track on a piece of paper by the bed. The next call there was no argument. Lane and Jenny were able to apply the principle of measurement to assess the truth. In a sense, their little piece of paper became their polygraph.

I know when I want to lose a few pounds I had better not trust my feelings about whether that late-night ice cream had an impact on my weight. I had better not trust my eyes either, because as I get older, I might look at the "skinny side" of me. Now, if I am serious, I get on the scale and weigh myself regularly. The scale is the only measure I trust. It's a fact that I weigh what I weigh. If I am serious about weight loss, I record my weight on a sticky note on my mirror.

Now, the sad or triumphant story of my weight saga is told in the brilliant colors of facts, not fantasy. I might fantasize that I am more or less, but the numbers on my sticky note keep me honest—and sometimes humble!

AVOID THE SAND TRAPS

How are you feeling at this point in the chapter? I hope you are still hanging in there. If you are, take a deep breath, because we have a bit more hiking to do.

I can hear some of you saying, "But you cannot measure what's on the inside." That's not true at all. You can measure your insides by your behavior.

Jesus said, "If you love me, you will obey what I command" (John 14:15). If we love Jesus, we obey what He commands. If we don't obey His commands, we don't perfectly love Him and may love ourselves a little too much.

As you measure yourself, you receive not only the benefit of operating on fact but another gift also. That gift is the gift of knowing where you truly are in comparison to your stated goals. Measurement removes all vagueness from your objectives.

I remember when I was working on my master's degrees in Texas and Lisa and I would go home for vacations to Pennsylvania. These drives home would take approximately twenty-four hours from Fort Worth, Texas, to Allentown, Pennsylvania. Now these trips all occurred before the Internet. (Yes, there was life before MapQuest.)

We would happily go to one place before we headed off for the very long dusty trail through Texas. We went to the AAA store to get our TripTik. This handy map outlined our entire trip. As we drove from city to city, state to state, we would flip the pages; each page would tell us where we were and how far until the next destination along the way.

These facts helped us make adjustments like food, gas, and bathroom stops, and they gave us an accurate positioning of our location to get there and get back to Texas. Being measured allows you to know where you are on your journey.

Measurement allows you to avoid the sand traps of fantasy, denial, false perception, and verbal reality on your journey to get a grip on your behavior.

The sand trap of fantasy

Fantasy allows you to live totally unaware of the reality you are in. Many people live in fantasy about their health, wealth, relationships, how they grew up, their sexual past, and parenting.

An example of this is a woman I know who had abandoned her two-year-old son to her ex-husband. She rarely visited after she moved away from him and lived many states away. The boy grew up, got into all kinds of trouble, and is sitting in a jail as I write this. She, however, thinks today that she was a good mom—now that's a fantasy!

The sand trap of denial

Denial is when you really do know the truth but refuse to admit it. You are overweight, compulsive, angry, and afraid, but you just plain pretend it is not true. "I'm not angry," you say while you yell at a child or spouse. Denial is when you know you don't have the money to pay the credit card, but you are spending like you can. Denial knows the status; it just ignores the facts.

The sand trap of false perceptions

Another sand trap is false perceptions. I remember somewhere in our marriage Lisa was repeatedly telling me that my hearing was getting bad, but I didn't think I was old enough to have hearing problems. This issue would come up again and again.

As a counselor, my hearing is critical while I work with people. I not only need to hear words, I need to hear nuances as well, especially with phone clients. As Lisa persisted about a possible problem with my hearing, I resorted to the facts.

I set up a hearing test. I made sure we went together so Lisa could hear the technician and help pick out the hearing aid if I needed one! I humbled myself to be measured. The technician fired off a bunch of beeps and buzzes and switched ears back and forth, and in a short time the computer gave the results. I had great hearing (except when it came to my wife). Being willing to say, "Measure me, please," ended Lisa's false perceptions and also silenced an argument that might have plagued our relationship for decades.

The sand trap of verbal reality

The last sand trap to avoid is verbal reality. *Verbal reality* is a term I coined that describes people who believe that if you say something, then it is true, and if you say it with feeling, it is *really* true.

If a man caught in the sand trap of verbal reality tells his wife, "I love you," he believes it must be true, especially if he says it with emotion. It doesn't matter that he won't work, is disrespectful, is physically abusive, and runs around on her with other women. This man doesn't love his wife: he is in verbal reality. He thinks that what he says is true, regardless of his behavior. But he couldn't be more wrong. You see, a person's behavior—not their speech—reveals the truth of what is really going on inside of them.

YOU CAN'T CHANGE WHAT YOU DON'T MEASURE

That's why the scale, the bank account, or other tools of measurement are really important. If you want to buy a house or car, you might think, hope, wish, and pray that you have a credit rating that will make it possible. But a credit report will give you the facts. It provides you with a black-and-white credit score that tells you if you are ready to buy a large ticket item at a reasonable rate of interest.

I know it can be hard, but when you are trying to get a grip on your life, facts are your friends! They are measures of how you are doing. Facts are like those guides you drive your car into when you get your car washed. They keep you in the middle so the process can work.

Most of us don't mind being measured when we know we have been successful. What man who has a twenty-inch arm fears the tape measure? What average-weight woman fears the scale? What responsible multimillionaire fears checking in with his accountant? You know as well as I do that it is human nature to want to look good.

In your life, there are probably several areas where measurement would be awesome. We humans are like that; we all have areas where we shine stunningly, and, if measured, it would simply affirm that we have an area of our life under control.

Measuring our weakness is what we often avoid. *Oh no, let's not do that. I won't look so good,* we tell ourselves. I know that if I binged the night before on nachos, ice cream, soda, or candy, I do not exactly want to jump on the scale the next morning. I would rather wait a day or two, and then I might feel better to place my feet on that "fact teller," the scale.

What if I struggle with envy, pride, self-righteousness, superiority, unkindness, or impatience? Then these will be areas where I will try to avoid being measured by others, God, His Word, or myself. (No, I don't want to hear that love is patient when just yesterday it took an hour and a half to drive six miles on a Los Angeles highway!)

When I am weak, I tend to want to hide. That is exactly the worst thing I can do, but it is the first thing I want to do. It is like riding a four-wheeler, also called an all-terrain vehicle (ATV). When an ATV starts leaning, your natural instinct is to put your foot out to stop this huge machine from falling, but this course of action will snap your leg like a twig. Instead, safety experts agree that even though you will not be able to stop the ATV from tipping, it is safer to ignore your instinct, keep your leg in, and roll with the vehicle.

In the same way, when we are struggling with something in our lives, it is safer to ignore our instinct to hide it. We have to listen to the experts who tell us that it is better to allow ourselves to be measured if we want to get a grip on what is controlling us.

HOW TO CREATE A MEASURE FOR YOUR LIFE

So now let's talk about how to create a measure for your life. For some, finding a way to measure their behavior is as easy as looking at the scale or the bank account at the end of the month. For others, it is more complex. It begins with identifying the inward beliefs that are causing the outward behaviors. For instance, envy might show itself in talking about others (gossip), putting others down, or finding the negative in a person or situation.

I remember Lisa and I bought our first house while I was still in seminary. The Lord had blessed us, and it was a really nice house to us—brand-new, never lived in. We were so excited. We had some friends over even before we had furniture to fill it.

Instead of the normal *oohing* and *ahhing*, one of the individuals focused on how the front door had glass in it and could easily be broken into. He struggled with envy, so putting a damper on someone's joy was his consistent pattern of life.

It goes to show you how tricky it can be to measure yourself. A person with envy might not even realize that envy is the inward root of their problem. Instead they must evaluate their outward behavior. Instead of a checklist that they mark every time they are envious, this person might have to make a checklist to measure their envious behavior.

Table 11-1: Measure Yourself Sample: "Envy Log"

- ☐ I put people down today.
- ☐ I built people up today.
- ☐ I dampened others' successes.
- ☐ I celebrated and highlighted the success of others.
- ☐ I spoke negative things about others today.
- ☐ I told positive things about others today.
- ☐ I listened to or participated in gossip.
- ☐ I removed myself from gossip

After creating such a checklist, persons who are controlled by envy has a better chance at being successful. Now that they can measure each of these outward behaviors for their inner out-of-control issue (envy), they can be successful.

The same technique works for men who struggle with lust. I have counseled many men who struggle with this inward issue. They are faithful to their wives and avoid pornography but struggle regularly with lust—at the office, while running errands, and even at church. They feel badly about their lust and repent of it frequently. But lust is an inward issue at the root of outward behaviors that can be measured. At my counseling center, we call these measures a "Lust Log." When a man makes a "Lust Log," he might want to be specific.

Table 11-2: Measure Yourself Sample: "Lust Log"

- ☐ Did I objectify a woman?

- Did I look back at a woman?
- Did I scan a woman?
- Did I place my eyes on inappropriate body parts?
- Did I assess her physically?

This could be turned into key words like *objectify, back, scan, parts,* and *assess.* A man can put these words on an index card, and no one will know what they mean. As he goes through the day, he just checks the boxes as needed. It has been my experience that within a couple of weeks, he will begin to see significant progress in his behavior and with the issue of lust.

I can hear some of you ladies thinking that if he would just repent, he would stop doing that. I would suggest that he has probably repented hundreds of times and is just finding it difficult to change. Just like the woman who keeps spending or eating, she repents daily but doesn't get a grip on what is controlling her.

You can repent, wish, hope, and long to change, but you can't measure these desires. Behavior can be measured, and you are much more likely to be successful if you measure it. Let me give you some examples.

Cindy had a real problem with gossip. She lost several boyfriends and female friends because of her problem. Cindy was twenty-nine and attractive but had never married. It seemed that once she knew someone well enough, she would find their weakness, turn on them, and expose their weakness to others, especially people in her church. She had started to realize the negative consequences of her behavior and came to me for help. She had repented regularly about gossiping, exaggerating, and even lying about others who were close to her. She could see and feel the chaos she was creating for herself and others.

Even throughout counseling she could see how her dad did this to the children and how much she didn't like it back then, but she would still find herself out of control with gossiping. To measure her behavior, we decided to have Cindy make some goals for how she would handle her behavior of sharing negative information about others. Here was Cindy's first set of goals for herself.

1. If she saw anything negative, she was to write it down in her prayer journal, date it, and pray for that person for seven days from her discovery.
2. If she said anything negative or exposing about another person, she had twenty-four hours to ask that person to forgive her.
3. When anyone started to gossip about another person, she was to make a positive statement about the person they were discussing.

Here is what Cindy learned in her first few weeks of measuring herself. She found that she spent too much time seeing the negative. She sometimes was praying up to twenty minutes for seven days for people.

She also realized that she really hated humbling herself and asking forgiveness, although she found that people respected her more when she did. She also found that in about a month she was able to more regularly say positive things about others, which kept the conversation from spiraling into a gossip session.

She wasn't fixed totally in a month's time. She made several more goals and utilized some of the principles in the future chapters. She did, however, stop, and at age thirty-one she was married to a great Christian man.

Jed was controlled by computer games. He always had the latest and best games. His friends nicknamed him the "Gamester." Jed was thirty-four and an engineer by day. But at night he was the Gamester. He would play games with real people, computer opponents, and people on the Internet.

Jed was getting increasingly more isolated; he had few friends and no woman in his life for seven years. It seemed there were very few women who wanted to play or watch video games for hours at a time until late in the evening.

Jed was in conflict. He loved his gaming but wanted so desperately to date and have a family. He would actually cry when talking about wanting a family. Finally, Jed was willing to make some measurable goals for his activities.

1. He could not play any games until 10:00 p.m. each night.
2. He had to rotate a schedule of going to exercise or get together with someone and do something. He set up Monday, Wednesday, and Friday as workouts after work; Tuesday, Thursday, and Saturday for social activities; and Sunday he was at church.
3. He could only play one game per week. All other games had to stay at his parents' home.
4. He blocked all Internet game sites.

The first three weeks of measuring these goals were hell for Jed. He told me he had wasted time from 9:30 p.m. to 10:00 p.m. for two nights. He just sat and watched the minutes go by. He wanted to cheat on the Internet at work so badly—and actually did three times.

On the positive, he lost seven pounds by going to the gym, mountain biking, and hiking. He attended every singles event at his church and got the calendar for the singles events from another large church in town.

He felt silly still going to his parents and switching the games out. Although he was doing better, he made more goals to measure and applied a few of the other principles to get a grip on his life.

Six months later, Jed was much better. He felt he could say no to games and actually had a period of twelve days where he had no gaming. He still wasn't married, but he had been able to go on a few dates and was actually blossoming in a Christian singles group.

Both Cindy and Jed had to measure their goals in order to see themselves honestly and change. It wasn't easy, and both Cindy and Jed made adjustments and refinements to their plan to get a grip on what was controlling them.

All right now, enough talk about measurement—we need to get right to work. You already know of one or more behaviors that have gotten control over your life. Let's list the top three below.

Table 11-3: Behaviors That Control Me

My behavior A is: ______________________________

My behavior B is: ______________________________

My behavior C is: ______________________________

Measures for Behavior A. I believe I can assess my behavior by the following behaviors:

1. ______________________________
2. ______________________________
3. ______________________________
4. ______________________________
5. ______________________________

Measures for Behavior B. I believe I can assess my behavior by the following behaviors:

1. ______________________________
2. ______________________________
3. ______________________________

4. ____

5. ____

Measures for Behavior C. I believe I can assess my behavior by the following behaviors:

1. ____

2. ____

3. ____

4. ____

5. ____

Remember, as I stated earlier in this book, you may have more than three behaviors to work on; however, I would caution you not to try to get a grip on too many behaviors at once. Three is the maximum that most people can handle at one time. Actually, some people find it much more successful to attack one behavior at a time. You decide what your approach should be for you to get a grip on what is controlling you.

Measurement is an essential part of getting a grip on what is controlling you. Unfortunately it is not the only step to getting control, but with a few more ingredients you will be able to structure a successful journey for you to get a grip on what is controlling you. Let's turn the page to discover our seventh step.

Chapter Twelve

Step 7: The Power-up Principle

Session after session, year after year, my clients share their successes and their failures with me. Being an eternal student, I love to learn from other people. Lisa, my wife, also loves to learn from people.

Lisa is the last of six children. She watched her siblings growing up and saw them make good choices and less-than-wonderful choices. She still learns from her siblings as they enter the next stage of life ahead of her. Learning from others is a great part of the human journey for those who are open-hearted.

I learned something from a thirty-one-year-old client named Shawn. Although he had a great wife, three children, taught Sunday school to sixth-grade boys in his church, and was a professional in his field of work, Shawn had a behavior that was controlling his life. He would buy lottery tickets, go to casinos, and bet on football and basketball games. He had stretches where he was ahead, and he had stretches where he was behind.

His gambling caused a couple of rocky years for him and his wife, Elaine. The couple had almost divorced and also almost went bankrupt.

Then Shawn became a Christian. Shortly after, Elaine also met Jesus, and life became much easier all around.

They stayed married and both worked hard to pay all their debts. Shawn started a company, and in three years he was making a lot of money. Then Shawn started to invest obsessively in the stock market. First it was small, and he generally made some money; then he started putting bigger money into his trading. He was on the computer for hours a day doing this.

His marriage and money were being impacted just like before. He would lie about trading to his wife. He would trade on margins and had to take out a home equity loan to cover it. That's when he started to seek help.

Shawn was able to work most of the principles that I shared in the last chapter in order to get a grip on what was controlling him. He was quick to ask forgiveness and disclose his sins, tried to put some positive behaviors into practice, and he didn't even mind some measurement in his recovery process. The one step Shawn wouldn't apply was the "power-up" principle I am about to share.

Once Shawn applied this principle I'm about to share into his process, he was able to get a grip on his gambling and spending. Now he is again not only successful but also stable and in full control of what was controlling him.

Sheila was a twenty-nine-year-old single mother. She worked in a large ministry. Sheila was quick to smile, energetic, attractive, and healthy. Sheila had a history of bad choices but seemed to have a way to rebound from what chaos she created in her life or just the circumstances she was in.

Sheila, although a Christian, had a nagging behavior that had control over her entire life. Sheila deeply struggled with lying. She would flat out lie to people in her life about what she was doing, where she was, whom she was with, and what she was doing.

Sheila had a way to tell a story about visiting her brother for the weekend when that wasn't remotely what she did. She had fictitious friends who had large houseboats, and she even "met some famous people." The problem was none of these events or people were true. Sad to say, she would do this in front of her six-year-old daughter who would get confused when they didn't go to these places but rather stayed home, watched television, and ate macaroni and cheese.

Sheila was colorful to listen to. She, like Shawn, was able to ask forgiveness, disclose, start positive behaviors, and measure herself for the most part. She, like Shawn, just didn't want to power up. She was slow to see and to sense her need for powering up. Once her little girl caught her when she was not being honest, and it caused the child to cry excessively. It was then that she powered up and really got control of the lying that was controlling her life.

So as I said before, I really like learning from people. What I have learned from many people's stories is that without powering up, most don't fully get a grip on what is controlling their life.

So let's talk about powering up. I am sure by now you are slightly curious as to what this seventh step in our journey is all about. Powering up is a principle that can make the difference between failure and success.

THE POWER-UP PRINCIPLE

I want to take you to a passage in the Bible that gives us the foundation for the power-up principle.

> Two are better than one,
>
> because they have a good return for their work:
>
> If one falls down,
>
> his friend can help him up.
>
> But pity the man who falls
>
> and has no one to help him up!
>
> —Ecclesiastes 4:9–10

Here we see the first principle of powering up: two are better than one. I have seen countless people try to get a grip on what was controlling them by themselves. They try, and they push, but they still end up just failing one more time. Being creatures that want to figure out something, we sometimes come to the wrong conclusions.

We alone try, and we fail; we try alone, and we fail again. So what most conclude is that it is not possible to get a grip on what is controlling us. But that's the wrong conclusion. A better conclusion is that you can't get a grip on this area of your life by yourself.

I'll never forget a classic conversation I had with Sam. Sam was a bright man, married, churchgoing, and fun to be around. Sam had a sexual addiction. As I advise all my sex-addicted clients, they must attend a support group so they can power up to be successful.

Sam really, really had reservations about this. He said if he could just meet with me; it would work better. "What if somebody knows me?" he contended. Sam definitely didn't want to go to a group and muscle up. So I asked Sam if he was a man of his word. He said yes, so I made Sam a deal.

"Sam," I said, "if you can stay free from the sexual behavior by just seeing me, you don't have to go to group."

Sam looked prematurely relieved. I continued, "If, however, you have one slip, you go to group. Do we have a deal?"

He agreed.

Sure enough, when I saw Sam a week later, he had slipped. But he kept his word and went to group. Sam experienced freedom from sexual addiction as he powered up.

Powering up means you let others really help you. If you are stuck in quicksand, struggling harder and harder by yourself doesn't help you to get out of the quicksand. Rather, if someone throws you a rope and you allow his or her strength to pull you up, you are much better off.

I remember a very vivid incident in my life where having others help me was very important. I was probably around twelve years old when this incident happened to me. I was walking my dog Caesar. Caesar was a very large German shepherd. We lived by many acres of cornfields with a dirt road where I would walk the dog behind our house. It had been raining regularly for the last week, so I was ready to go outside. My mom made me wear my black rubber rain boots, the kind with metal latches on them.

While walking with Caesar, I got the idea to walk through the cornfield that had been harvested instead of walking on the road. I would do this occasionally and let Caesar off his leash to run around as dogs like to do. We walked quite far into the very muddy field. I walked into an area that was so muddy I actually couldn't move. I was physically not strong enough to get myself out of the mud. I was stuck for quite some time, sitting in the mud. Caesar couldn't help; he had more sense than to come near me. He ran around and then left.

After a while, I saw my stepdad walking toward me with Caesar running around him. My stepdad made some wisecrack about my situation (as any dad might) and then reached down and pulled me up out of my boots. I walked home with probably the dirtiest socks ever in sock history.

I needed to power up. I didn't have the power within myself. I had to rely on the strength of another to pull me out of what was controlling my life. My efforts just got me nowhere but more frustrated and dirtier.

So if you plan to go it alone again, before you do, I want you to really think about this. How many times have you tried your way? Fill in the chart below.

Table 12-1: Past Attempts to Get a Grip

Write down how often you tried by yourself to get a grip on what is controlling you.

Behavior 1

Year I tried ________ Results ____________________________________

Year I tried ________ Results ____________________________________

Year I tried ________ Results ____________________________________

Year I tried ________ Results ____________________________________

Year I tried ________ Results ____________________________________

Behavior 2

Year I tried ________ Results ________________________________

Year I tried ________ Results ________________________________

Year I tried ________ Results ________________________________

Year I tried ________ Results ________________________________

Year I tried ________ Results ________________________________

Behavior 3

Year I tried ________ Results ________________________________

Year I tried ________ Results ________________________________

Year I tried ________ Results ________________________________

Year I tried ________ Results ________________________________

Year I tried ________ Results ________________________________

Now honestly look at the results. If you see a pattern of failure, why would you want to try your alone plan again? Honestly, that might not be the best idea for you if you really want to get a grip on what is controlling you.

If we believe Einstein's definition that *insanity* is doing the same thing but expecting a different result, then it stands to reason that the definition for *sanity* would be trying something different to get different results. If you have traveled the path alone for years, how about trying something radically different, such as allowing a person or people to help you get a grip on what is controlling you?

ACCOUNTABILITY

The second principle of powering up is accountability. Let me remind you of James 5:16: "Therefore confess your sins to each other and pray for each other so that you may be healed. The prayer of a righteous man is powerful and effective."

You see, for us to heal we must confess our faults to each other. I know absolutely that if I want healing, I have to confess my faults to someone. If I keep my faults and shortcomings to myself, it is a path to having something control me. Years have gone by since many things have controlled me. By the grace of God and applying these principles in this book, I have been able to get a grip on many things that had previously controlled my life.

I didn't like this principle any more than Sam, whom we talked about earlier. I thought telling someone else would just cause me to be rejected; however, I discovered the opposite to be true. I felt *more* loveable, not *less*.

I find it interesting that Scripture tells us to "confess our faults" (James 5:16, KJV). It is amazing to me that it presumes we will have faults. It does not say, "*If* you have faults," but rather tells us what to do with them *when* we have them.

We all have faults—anger, pride, rudeness, worthlessness, fear, spending, substances, food, or hundreds of others that are possible. If we power up and actually become accountable to someone, we can finally get a grip on what has been controlling us.

Becoming accountable to someone is not an *instant* healing; it is a *process* of healing. Over time, with consistent and real accountability, you get stronger. Reaching your behavioral goals becomes easier and easier. Before you know it, your accountability is revealing more of you being in control of your behavior than of it controlling you.

THE STRUCTURE OF ACCOUNTABILITY

Now let's talk about the structure of your accountability. The first thing you need to do is discuss the negative behaviors with your primary person. Tell them exactly what has control over your life. Be brave—the embarrassing part is short-lived, but the freedom can be lifelong.

It's like the vaccinations most babies receive. The temporary pain from the needle is quickly over, but the resistance to disease is lifelong. Before we go any further, let's look at two examples.

Robert was struggling with vanity. He was an attractive-looking thirty-year-old in great shape, which he would talk about repeatedly and at length. He worked in a twenty-four-hour gym as one of the lead fitness trainers. Robert was able to state what was controlling him (vanity) and sincerely wanted Christ to be seen in him more than vanity. Robert made the following three behavioral goals.

1. Not to turn a conversation toward his physical appearance
2. Not to flex or pose in front of a mirror (this was a daily ritual)
3. To wear a regular T-shirt at work and when working out

These were Robert's first three goals. He decided to make Marc (another trainer) his primary person. Marc was twenty-four, newly married, and a Christian for about two years. Robert told Marc he was struggling with some pride issues and wanted to meet for breakfast on Thursdays to go over his goals.

Marc and Robert met, and the first two to three meetings went well. Robert went over the goals and really was doing pretty good. By the fourth meeting, the conversation went more like, "So how are you doing?" and then the two trainers would wolf down some Egg Beaters omelets, talk about "the biz," and generally shoot the breeze.

Slowly Robert began to shift back to some old behaviors. The Spirit pricked him one morning when he was posing after taking a shower that he needed more accountability. After talking about this, Robert picked Rock, a fifty-five-year-old, large farmer-type who was the men's ministry leader. Rock had been married for more than thirty years with four grown kids and had a "countrified wisdom" about him. Rock was able to help Robert stay on track.

Marcia also had a behavior that was controlling her life. Marcia was unable to say no to her mother and her adult daughter. She found herself exhausted, running her mother to appointments (her father could still drive), and watching the grandchildren a few nights a week, while trying to run her and her husband's company as well.

Marcia was able to clearly identify what was controlling her (having no boundaries with all the women in her family) and made three distinct behavioral goals.

1. I can only drive mother to appointments on Mondays; all other days are off limits.
2. I will only watch grandchildren from 4:00 p.m. to 8:30 p.m. on Thursday night.
3. I will run every request for my time through my primary person before I say yes to females in my family.

Marcia was really nervous about her goals. They seemed so cold and selfish to her. She agreed to meet with their pastor's wife, Diane, who was about five years her senior and whom she had known for about sixteen years.

Diane and Marcia met together every other week faithfully for "tea" at Diane's house. Marcia kept her goals on one index card. On another index card she actually kept a scorecard. Here was her scorecard.

Table 12-2: Measure Yourself Scorecard Sample: "Marcia"

	1	2	3	4	5	6	7	8	9	10	11	12	13	14
1. Mondays														

2. Thursdays														
3. Run request by Diane														

When Marcia and Diane met they agreed the first thing they would discuss was Marcia's scorecards. In the beginning, Marcia had a few slips with her daughter and not calling Diane as she should have. It took about six weeks for Marcia to get a perfect score.

Marcia was so pleased with her "new life." She was now able to go for walks and have regular dates with her husband. Her accountability with Diane was working. Marcia liked the process and the results so much she talked Diane into a second behavior she wanted to get a grip on.

Of course, Marcia and Diane had chitchatted over their tea, but that came *after* the two women went over Marcia's card. Actually, Diane started a goal herself the second time, and now both are getting a grip on something in their lives.

For accountability to work, you must:

1. **Be specific:** Robert told his primary person that he was working on pride, not vanity. Marcia was clear that it was a lack of boundaries. The more specific you are about your goal, the better your chances to get a grip on your life.

2. **Focus your accountability:** Robert was willing to let the focus of their meeting become vague and undirected. Marcia had her cards and talked about her behavior goals before they poured the tea.

3. **Have a period of success:** Marcia waited until she was in control for more than six months before she discontinued the focus of her first behavior.

IT'S YOUR TURN

Now let's make a decision before we go any further. In the space below, rewrite the behaviors for which you need accountability in order to help you get a grip on what is controlling you.

Behavior One: ______________________________

Behavior Two: ______________________________

Behavior Three: ______________________________

Now, take another minute and decide in what order these behaviors are best to be addressed. What behavior do you want to address first? Some people choose the most difficult behavior to start with, and others choose the easiest one. Regardless of which behavior you want to address first, write them below in order of priority.

Behavior One: ______________________________

Behavior Two: ______________________________

Behavior Three: ______________________________

There is an important decision you have to make before you can get a grip on the behavior controlling you. You have to decide whether you will be fully accountable to another person. You have to decide that you are absolutely done with the idea that you are going to do it all by your "almighty self." It is time to ask yourself if you are willing to be accountable to another person with the behavior you listed as your top priority. Check your answer below.

- ☐ Yes, I am willing to be accountable on my first behavior to get a grip on what is controlling me.
- ☐ No, I am not willing to be accountable on my first behavior to get a grip on what I say I want control over.

______________________ ______________________

(sign here) *(date)*

One more question needs to be addressed before we go any further with accountability. Are you willing to be accountable until you have six months of being in control over what has been controlling you? Now look carefully at what I just asked you. I did not ask if you would be accountable for six months. What I asked you was if you would be willing to be accountable for six months where you have been successful at controlling the behavior that in the past has been controlling you. This might take nine months, a year, or longer. Are you willing to persist until the mission is accomplished? Below state your objective.

- ☐ Yes, I am 100 percent committed to accountability until I am in control of what has been controlling me for six months.
- ☐ No, I am not committed to accountability until I am successful for six months of getting a grip on what is controlling me.

______________________	______________________
(sign here)	*(date)*

OK, if you have signed off to the "yes" answers in the last two questions you can proceed on with the chapter and the rest of the book. I will warn you: it is still an uphill climb from here, but the view is so worth it. To see the absolute beauty of your success is absolutely worth the journey. This beauty is why I keep counseling people. Week after week I see lives turned around and people able to get freer than they have been most of their life. The beauty of being set free from a controlling behavior is absolutely glorious to see.

For those of you who are not committed to accountability, I encourage you to read on. It will be important for you to know the principles to get a grip on what is controlling you. You can be used also to help others get a grip on what has been controlling them. I will warn you, though, as they come back with their success stories and thanking you there may be a time you will consider turning your own "no" to "yes."

To the brave souls that are in for a new experience of getting a grip on what is controlling you, I say congratulations. If you follow through with your accountability, you can finally get control back into your life. You are now ready to get powered up!

There are a few issues I want to help clarify with you in your power-up process so that you can be laser sharp as you get a grip on what has been controlling you. The first issue we need to address is to whom you want to make yourself accountable. For a complete list of characteristics that are especially important to look for in choosing a primary person who will hold you accountable, refer back to chapter nine. In that chapter I gave you what I think are some general principles that can be very helpful. Below is a recap of that list. Feel free to add characteristics that are especially important to you.

1. Honest
2. Trustworthy
3. Available
4. Accepting
5. Not family
6. Spiritually mature
7. Professional
8. Other ______________________
9. Other ______________________
10. Other ______________________

As you look at this list, there is one other characteristic that I find helpful. You may want to consider adding it to the list. I find it helpful for my primary person to have success in the area in which I need to grow. I know this is not always possible, but it is a great characteristic to keep in mind.

Take a moment and think through the list of people you know who can help you with behavior number one on your list of these things that control you. You can think through friends, people you know from church, support groups, or others. As you think about this, you may also want to pray and ask God who would be best for you to be accountable to.

Usually you will have a peace about the right person as you go through this process of choosing someone. Remember, there is no perfect person except Jesus. So you get to pick from people who are flawed but loved just like yourself.

After taking time to pray and think about whom you should make yourself accountable to, it is time to ask them. You could simply ask this person directly: "Kate, I am setting some goals to improve ____________ area of my life. I need some accountability to make sure I stay focused. Can I call or get together with you to help me for the next several months?" Once a person has agreed to become your primary person, place his or her name in the following space. You may want a different person as your primary person for different behaviors in your life.

Table 12-3: Primary Person Selection

Behavior 1: ________________________________

Behavior 2: ________________________________

Behavior 3: ________________________________

A second issue to address is stating the exact time commitment you are asking of this person. I recommend that you ask him or her to commit to get together with you once a week or every other week.

Less than that can be ineffective for you to get enough out of your accountability and be successful in getting a grip on this behavior.

The other request you will need to ask is that when you meet, you will first review your behavioral goals and your current measurement. You are committing to be totally honest, even if you fail. You may also ask that part of your accountability be that you pray together before you conclude your meeting.

Stating exactly what you are asking of your primary person gives them the best opportunity to help you. As you utilize this accountability, you will begin to feel the benefits of what I call powering up.

Once you have selected the behavior, the measure, and the accountability, you are well on your way to the top of the mountain. I do have to tell you there is one more step to take. Like mountain climbing in Colorado, most times the path gets tougher as you travel. So read the next chapter, and then we will put it all together so you can get the maximum out of your journey.

Chapter Thirteen

Step 8: "Spank the Dog"

"Welcome to the last part of the journey," the guide says as the group looks up to the summit of the climb. Several thoughts go through your mind as you stare at the intimidating mountain peak. You notice that it is a difficult climb—almost straight up—and you are not sure if you will walk or get down on all fours to make it to the top.

You are exhausted from the five-and-a-half-hour journey it took you to climb to this point. *Are you kidding?* you think. *Do I really want to climb these boulders with no apparent path? Who talked me into this? Do I want to lose all my pride and say I can't do it? What would this group of friends and strangers think? Can I claim I can't breathe because the air is so thin?* These and several other thoughts race through your mind right before those dreadful words come out of your mouth: "Let's go!"

That's exactly how you might feel as we take the eighth and final step in our process of getting a grip. I call this step *Spank the Dog.* I know you are probably thinking, *What does that mean?*

I have the same reaction when we go white-water rafting and the guide directs us around the corner and points at a group of rocks and says, "There's a shark's tooth," or "There's an Indian chief." At first glance you only see a rock, but if you let his words create the picture, you begin to see the shark's tooth or Indian chief.

Well, let me be your guide through these waters. I have been through these waters many times. Our adventure starts with a very old theory derived from man's best friend.

Everyone knows who a man's best friend is, right? His dog. That's right, somewhere in ancient times, dogs became pets to mankind. Dogs were loveable, entertaining, and helpful. Men depended on dogs to help them hunt, and they utilized dogs as early "alarm systems" to warn them of predators entering their territories.

This bond between people and dogs continues today. Dogs are unquestionably great creatures, but unfortunately they do come with one incredible deficit. These benevolent creatures we love to love have accidents. These cute little fuzz balls that we just want to kiss—and maybe even be kissed by—have accidents in the kitchen, on the rugs (regardless of how expensive they are), hardwood floors, and slate. Oh yes, and they have all different kinds of accidents.

Throughout history, I am sure that dog owners wrestled with what to do about this problem, and then, *eureka!* On the day newspapers were invented, the answer became clear. You roll up the newspaper, and when Fuzzy has an accident, you spank the dog. It works! For more than one hundred years, people across the world have solved their doggy dilemmas with the spank-the-dog solution.

Now dogs, being sensitive creatures that want to avoid this most uncomfortable feeling, have learned to refrain from having accidents in the dwellings of their owners. They have learned to find "no-spank zones" somewhere outside to utilize instead.

NOBODY LIKES PAIN

Now let me take the paradigm of Spank the Dog, break it down, and apply it to this final step in our journey to get a grip on out-of-control behavior in our lives. The reason Spank the Dog works is because pain avoidance trains more than dogs. Nobody likes pain. We try to avoid pain at all costs.

That's why God has allowed many consequences for improper behavior to be painful. Try touching fire. Just the thought of that makes you think, *No way, that hurts.* Some of us learned that one the hard way. How about going eighty miles an hour in a fifty-five-mile zone with a police officer sitting under the bridge? Oh, that's painful, especially if your spouse has been sleeping on the seat next to you and is awakened by the police sirens! You don't forget the bridge or the speed limit for quite a while!

I'm sure you get the idea—pain makes you stop doing things. As a counselor looking for ways to help people break out of the control of addictive behaviors, I saw the value in this principle, but I doubted if people would take too kindly to being swatted with a rolled-up newspaper when their out-of-control behavior got the best of them! So one day when I was in my office and a sincere man asked how he should get rid of lustful thoughts, a technique one of my professors taught me about something else popped into my mind. The man in my office was lusting or objectifying women. He didn't want to do this, but felt helpless against his behavior. When he asked me for help, I got up, went to the outer office, and came back with the secret weapon for lust: *a rubber band.*

You are probably thinking, *How does a rubber band become a secret weapon against lust?* Well, that's what my client thought as well. I instructed my client to place the rubber band on his wrist, and every time he lusted, he was to snap his wrist with the rubber band. He did what his therapist said. Within a few weeks he reported that his lustful thoughts were reduced significantly.

I decided to call this technique Spank the Dog. Instead of his brain getting a rush for lusting, it was now getting pain. Even after just a few days, the brain began to want to avoid lusting. You might think this is off the wall, but it really works.

I did a survey years ago involving two thousand sexually addicted men. I asked them several questions in the survey. One of the questions was, "What has been most helpful in your recovery?" I didn't have any lists or boxes for the respondents to check off. I wanted them to tell me in their own words.

Tell us they did! The rubber band came in second place in our survey. The rubber band ranked above counseling, support groups, books, and others. This is a great testimony to the Spank the Dog principle.

In case you're still not sure what I'm talking about, I'll explain it this way. Whatever is controlling your life can be defined by behaviors. Once you identify these behaviors and take the first seven steps of our process for getting a grip on these behaviors, you can also assign a negative consequence to the out-of-control behaviors. Yes, I am suggesting that you set up a negative consequence for the behavior you wish to control.

Joe was forty-eight and married to a great woman with two wonderful children. Joe came from a family in which the men tended to die of heart attacks at about fifty years of age. Joe was also about eighty pounds overweight.

Joe had an office job, so he wasn't very physically active during the day. Neither did he work out when he was off the clock. Joe identified a behavior that contributed to his being overweight: he had developed a habit of having a post-dinner meal.

Joe would stay up until about midnight every night. Then right around ten to ten thirty, he would hit the fridge and the freezer for a little refreshment to go along with his television entertainment. He would eat some leftover meat loaf along with whatever else he could find. He also made sure he had a few scoops of his favorite ice cream. (Actually, all of them were his favorites.) Joe was consuming anywhere from one to three thousand calories during this late-night fourth meal and doing nothing else but sitting and sleeping.

Joe didn't want to die, so one of his goals was not to eat after 6:00 p.m. He could drink all the water, coffee, or hot tea without sugar he wanted. Now remember this was Joe's goal, not the direction of a therapist or doctor. Joe was serious about getting a grip on what was controlling him. Joe identified his eating patterns—rather than his weight—as a goal.

Joe did fine for about five days, and then he slipped. Then Joe started slipping regularly. Joe didn't want to fail, so he decided to Spank the Dog. Joe agreed that if he ate anything past 6:00 p.m., he would do thirty minutes on the rowing machine immediately.

Joe did slip, but it only happened once. Joe hated that thirty minutes of sweating. The consequences or "spanking" Joe set up was not only the thirty minutes on the rowing machine; it also included fifteen minutes of cooling off and taking a shower. This also meant that Joe lost about an hour or more of watching television.

Joe obviously had several things that were controlling his life. He was able to reduce his intake in the evening, eventually to get more and better sleep, and to feel much better about his heart and overall health.

Karen was an energetic young lady who was recently married. Both Karen and her new husband were good Christians who really loved each other, but Karen had grown up in a very critical family who would point out the faults of others on a regular basis.

Although Karen experienced very little of this critical behavior in her dating, after marriage it was like a switch went off in her head. She started finding things wrong with Jeff. Although it is common for couples to see more weaknesses in their partners after marriage than before, Karen's fault-finding was constant.

She began to criticize, correct, and even demean Jeff. She was out with her girlfriends, and she was running Jeff down to them until one of them just asked, "Why did you marry him if he is so bad?" That question shot through Karen's heart, and when she went to the car, she wept aloud to God. She was doing the same thing her mom and dad did. It felt like a curse was going to keep continuing if she didn't get hold of her criticism.

As I counseled her, Karen was able to identify several behaviors that contributed to her criticism of Jeff. She was following the steps

I've outlined in this book but still regularly slipping into what was controlling her life.

Karen needed the Spank the Dog principle if she was going to be successful in getting a grip on what was controlling her. So she thought about what she could do for a consequence for her criticism. She paused for a few minutes and then smiled. She said, "I definitely know what will work."

"What?" I asked.

She said, "For every criticism of my husband, I will donate one dollar to the political party I don't vote for."

Since Karen was a very politically active person, this consequence would almost make her sick. To avoid it, Karen developed a kind way to bring up constructive criticism with Jeff. She learned to say, "I have an observation. Can I share it with you?" She used this introduction to address day-to-day differences any couple might go though, like how they fold clothes, load the dishwasher, and so on. After only four dollars, Karen was amazingly able to get a grip on her criticism. She disliked her one-dollar donations so much that she couldn't bring herself to continue this familiar behavior from her family history.

Joe and Karen are like so many of us who have something that has control over our lives. We are good people who want to get a grip on various areas of our lives. I mean, I can't count how many times I have lost the same ten pounds, so I can totally relate. Anytime I seriously want to lose those pounds again, I set up behaviors and consequences, and amazingly, after I Spank the Dog, the weight goes down.

Now, as Westerners, the idea of consequences is a foreign concept to many of us. Most of us live in a post-1960s' mentality that tells us there shouldn't be any consequences. What this mentality has done is set us up to become out of control and stay that way. The natural order of life has consequences, and this principle really works.

Let's take gravity for instance. Spank the Dog may have helped you to learn to respect gravity just as it did for me. I still have a scar on my right arm from jumping off of a roof after retrieving a Frisbee as a kid. Interestingly, I have never tested gravity since.

What about the consequences of breaking speed limits? Remember the first time those red and blue lights flashed behind you and those loud sirens went off. Remember how your heart rate went up, your chest pounded, and your hands got all clammy. Oh yeah, and who can forget that lovely conversation you had with your parents or your spouse about it afterwards. That was the natural order of consequences. It was Spank the Dog at its best.

For some, that first consequence was enough. For others it took several contributions to your city or state government. I lived in Texas for fifteen years. They had billboards everywhere for lawyers who could get you out of a traffic ticket. This promoted a life without speeding consequences. You only have to drive Texas highways for a short time to realize that most Texans have no fear of breaking the speed limit.

I know I'm spending extra time on this, but it is so critical for us to get a grip on our lives. I'll never forget Tony, a man who was so very out of control. His behavior had him risking AIDS several times a week. He had applied all of our steps and was in a support group for more than a year with absolutely no change in his behaviors.

Now I'd like to think I'm a great therapist, but all I did was explain the Spank the Dog principle. Tony agreed to a consequence that was distasteful to him and required him to wake up at 5:00 a.m. He slipped only once, and after that was able to get free from a behavior that had been controlling his life in a very large way.

I could tell you one hundred stories of how Spank the Dog has been successful in taking someone from "trying again" to getting a grip on what has been controlling them. You see, Spank the Dog puts real teeth to your desire to get a grip on what has been controlling you. You deserve to get a grip on what has been controlling you. You deserve to be absolutely free for the rest of our life.

Yet it's important to remember that the path to freedom isn't always pretty. It isn't always convenient. It isn't always conventional.

In John 9:6, Jesus spat on the ground, made mud, and put it on a blind man's eyes. I am absolutely sure that not one of the people standing around thought this method was conventional.

Conventionally you should have no consequences. Conventionally you should be able to do whatever you want. But what about Joe's case, when it could kill him, or Karen's situation, when it could have damaged a young marriage? I find that being outside the box, utilizing the power of consequences, or what I have been calling Spank the Dog, is a powerful way to finally get a grip on what has been controlling you.

WHO DECIDES THE CONSEQUENCE?

You might be asking yourself who gets to decide the consequence you'll face if you fall back into your old behavior. That's a very important question. Should you have your spouse, friend, or parent pick a consequence for you? I have not ever found that to work. How about a counselor or pastor then? When a spouse, friend, parent, or even a well-intentioned counselor or pastor sets the consequence, it is not pretty at all! After a relapse and consequence, it seems that all the negative emotion you feel about your consequence gets directed at the other person instead of yourself. So now because of your failure to keep a behavior goal, you are mad at your spouse, parent, friend, therapist, or pastor as if they did something; this just doesn't work.

You may consult others for their ideas, but never let anyone determine your consequence. You must decide it for yourself.

You see, you are an adult. I know in the area that has been controlling you, you might feel like you act like a child. It may even be true that when you are out of control you may be slightly more primitive in your emotions than a mature person in that area might be.

However, there's nothing like a jolt of a consequence to help you regain your sober mind. After Joe was committed to do the rowing machine, he was able to very soberly say no to his post-dinner meal. Karen was able to sober up and say no to her criticism of her husband.

Let me give you a practical example. Suppose that a person named Mace is struggling with lying, envy, and laziness. Mace is a twenty-three-year-old single male who wants to get a grip on his life. He decides his first behavior to deal with is his laziness. He sets three behavioral goals for himself.

1. To be out of bed by 8:00 a.m.
2. To be five minutes early for work
3. To complete whatever task he is working on before leaving work, staying up to fifteen minutes over if necessary

Now this isn't the first time Mace has set these kinds of goals for himself. His dread of even trying again can be seen all over his face. But this time he is able to architect some consequences. He understands this since he has a dog he has had to potty train in his one-bedroom apartment. So here are Mace's goals with consequences.

1. I will be out of bed by 8:00 am. My consequence is I will run two miles if the clock says 8:01 before I do anything else.

2. I will be five minutes early for work. My consequence is I will arrive thirty minutes early and not clock in until my scheduled time.

3. I will complete the task I'm working on before leaving work. My consequence is I will skip lunch the next day.

Mace was tired of being called lazy by his family of achievers and his last girlfriend who left him. So Mace went to the singles' pastor at his Methodist church. They agreed to touch base by phone weekly and have a catch up meeting every other Sunday before the Sunday evening singles' get together.

Mace and his pastor met for over eight months. Mace broke each of his goals, but he was faithful in doing his consequences. Mace did a great job picking his consequences; he didn't like working for free or running. Well after six times of running, Mace was able to get up at eight, and shortly he was on time and completed what he was working on at work.

Mace was committed to stopping his laziness. His accountability to his pastor made him more responsible. Mace gained confidence and was able to attack other out-of-control areas of his life.

Table 13-1: "Spank the Dog" Consequences Chart

So how about you? What is it going to be? Another, "Try again", or "OK, I'll try Spank the Dog." Check off the box that you agree with.

- ☐ I will try again with no consequence.
- ☐ I will try again with consequences.

Spank the Dog really works. I have seen it work for many people in my years of counseling. So let's get Spank the Dog to work for you. Below rewrite the top three behaviors that you have been working on to get a grip on in your life.

Behavior 1: ______________________________

Behavior 2: ______________________________

Behavior 3: ______________________________

As you have read previous chapters, you outlined your specific behavioral objectives to start getting a grip on your life. Now that you have listed your behaviors you want to control, let's review your behavioral goals for getting a grip on what is controlling you.

My behavior goals for Behavior 1 are:

1. ______________________________

____

2. ______________________________

____

3. ______________________________

____

My behavior goals for Behavior 2 are:

1. ____

____

2. ____

____

3. ____

____

My behavior goals for Behavior 3 are:

1. ____

____

2. ____

____

3. ____

____

At this point in the book you are really ready to take the final step to get a grip on what is controlling you. So below you can set up the power of Spank the Dog in your life by setting up consequences.

Behavior 1

My first behavioral goal: ______________________________

____

My consequence for this goal: ___________________________

____

My second behavioral goal: ____________________________

____

My consequence for this goal: ________________________________

____

My third behavioral goal: ________________________________

____

My consequence for this goal: ________________________________

____

Behavior 2

My first behavioral goal: ________________________________

____

My consequence for this goal: ________________________________

____

My second behavioral goal: ________________________________

____

My consequence for this goal: ________________________________

____

My third behavioral goal: ________________________________

____

My consequence for this goal: ________________________________

____

Behavior 3

My first behavioral goal: ________________________________

____

My consequence for this goal: ____________________________________

____

My second behavioral goal: ____________________________________

____

My consequence for this goal: ____________________________________

____

My third behavioral goal: ____________________________________

____

My consequence for this goal: ____________________________________

____

Now comes the fun part: pick the behavior you would like to start getting a grip on and commit to keeping your consequences. As you add the power of Spank the Dog to your life, your growth can take off exponentially. I have seen so many clients get a grip on what has been controlling them for decades, once they started applying Spank the Dog.

Remember, you are responsible before God to get a grip on your issues. Don't make your growth something that you do for another person. This life of freedom is for you. These are your battles; people can help and encourage you, but the battle to do what you have to do differently is in your capable hands. I wish you the best climbing you can have.

You can get a grip on what has been controlling you all these years. You can have a brighter future and relationships, and you are worth it.

Chapter Fourteen

The Big Picture

I don't know about you, but I like to know the big picture before I get started. I remember a thought I picked up from a motivational speaker (I can't recall who), but he said, "Start with the end in mind."

In other words, if you know where you are going, you will probably get there. I practically apply this with my hairdresser, Scott. Very occasionally (usually in the summer) I want a different haircut. So what I do is look in a few of the men's magazines and find a hairstyle I like. I remember one time a fellow whose haircut I liked was on the *Robb Report* magazine, and I had to buy a seven-dollar magazine just to get this picture to show Scott.

It was worth every penny. I showed Scott the picture and he said, "No problem." Scott got started with the end in mind and gave me the haircut I wanted.

In the same way, you can get a grip on what is controlling you. If you know what the end looks like, you will be able to get through the process to get there.

This idea of keeping the end in sight is something I use with any household project as well. When you are ripping out a sink or something fun like that, you better have a positive goal in mind. I personally find the "Law of Contracting" comes into play when I fix things. You know, that phenomenon when you've hired a contractor, but the project is twice as long and twice as much as you planned.

The same thing happens to me when I tackle do-it-yourself projects. But having what the project looks like at the end keeps me in the game whether things get interesting, bizarre, or tough.

Through this book I have tried to give you a clear picture of each part of the process. But if you've ever been to a gym, you know that the trainer will have you practice an exercise with no weight on it to warm you up and give your body a memory of the movement. I also want to walk you through the whole process so you have the big picture for yourself. As we move toward the end of the chapter, you will need a pen or pencil to write out for yourself from start to finish how you will get a grip on what has been controlling you.

But first I want you to meet Sal—a fifty-four-year-old divorcee who works as a maintenance man at a large church. Sal has been a Christian and has been "telling people about Jesus" for about two and a half years. He is a faithful member of his church, tithes, and works hard doing many things people don't see to make their Sunday and Wednesday services go off without a hitch.

Sal had a behavior that had been in control of his life since he was a teen. It didn't seem like a problem when he was in the military. When he left the military as a sergeant, he bartended, did construction, and maintenance, and it didn't seem like a problem then either.

It wasn't until he became a Christian and started to work around the church people that this became a noticeable pattern. What was his problem? He cursed. All the time. I mean, he could add a curse word to any sentence.

Yet in spite of this habit, everyone who met Sal liked him. He was a big-hearted and generous soul. He knew he was loved by God and his pastor, who said, "Sal, you have a good heart with a rough tongue, and we will take that heart any day." So he wasn't rejected or shamed in any way by his employer, but the Holy Spirit was starting to convince Sal that cursing wasn't a part of blessing God with his mouth.

So Sal went on a quest to get a grip on what was controlling him. First he memorized a cluster of scriptures that furthered his conviction, but he still didn't stop the behavior. Second, he asked a counselor in his congregation who told Sal to shout the word *Stop!* in his head after he cursed, but it didn't seem to have much of an affect on him.

Sal was sincere and discouraged when he walked through my door. Even in telling his dilemma he came close to cursing a few times in frustration. Sal wanted to get a grip on the cursing that was controlling his life.

Sal was willing to try some new ideas for his life, so we went step-by-step through the process. First we discussed the issue of self-honesty and any secrets Sal might be harboring.

Sal was very brave here in being self-honest. He discussed how his mom wanted a girl for her third child, and she was going to name her Sally. He was very ashamed of this because he was a man's man type. He discussed his dad's physical abuse, verbal abuse, drinking, and how he cheated on his mom. He shared his early sexual encounters that led to the abortion of a child. He shared his own drinking problem that led into a shameful sexual encounter he was plagued with having never told anyone. He shared about his marriage and parenting and how he became more like his dad as he aged.

Sal's self-honesty was a very critical step in getting a grip on what was controlling him. Sal, by his behavior, was clear in his decision to get a grip on the cursing that was controlling his life.

Sal's decision to get a grip on his cursing behavior also led him through the cleansing the temple exercise. He had anger toward his dad that he had to face. When he did this, he was able to place the abuse and his dad's shame for adultery that he carried for years. When Sal came out of this session he was sweating tremendously, but he really felt resolve.

Sal also did the cleansing the temple exercise with his mom for not accepting him as a boy and not protecting him from his dad's abuse. Sal also had anger with his ex-wife who left him for another man. Needless to say, these were the big problems, but Sal also had some other secrets to heal from, as many who walk through this process do.

Then we went to the next step for Sal to get a grip on what was controlling him. He had to forgive. I first worked with Sal on forgiving himself. He sat there for more than thirty minutes asking for forgiveness and crying as he pushed through the pain from his past, and he was able to forgive himself from his heart. It was evident by his face he had never really forgiven himself. He then was in a richer way able to accept God's forgiveness. An interesting comment he made was, "I feel like a real Christian." I asked him about this, and he said he never really felt like a Christian with all the anger he had in his heart and his obvious inability to forgive. He said, "I can't explain it, but it's like my heart feels clean."

Yes, even though he had accepted Christ, he always felt kind of grungy from his past. After Sal did some work, he was beginning to feel the roots of his cursing drying up. He wasn't as easily frustrated because he wasn't harboring pent-up anger anymore.

Disclosure wasn't that hard for Sal. He went through the big stuff early, but he did find some other issues as he did a complete enchilada story. Sal was an honest type, so he didn't feel that just telling me was good enough, "After all, I am paying you." He knew one other person who absolutely accepted him and could "handle it." So he made an appointment to see his pastor. The men met for a long time, and when Sal was done, Pastor Charlie was so proud of Sal he was crying. The two men prayed, and Sal was right—Pastor Charlie really did love him.

Sal was still slipping in his cursing, so we started to put the positive behaviors into play. Sal started his five behaviors of praying in the morning, reading, meeting with two guys at work with whom he regularly had lunch with, daily calling a single friend of his, and praying again at the end of the day as well. Sal commented, "Boy, I didn't realize I would have to work so hard to get better."

Sal activated these positive behaviors consistently and also began to measure his behavior. He had one of those really small spiral notebooks, the kind that fit in a shirt pocket. In the front he kept his daily assignments for his maintenance job. In the back he kept a daily log of his swearing. He separated cursing at objects (like stubborn pipes) and cursing in front of people.

Sal's measurement results were interesting. He cursed six times more at objects than at people. He was encouraged at this, but he had to get a grip on all his cursing since that was his goal—"to have a mouth that pleased the Lord who saved him."

Sal made himself accountable to Ralph, a retired man who actually volunteered on the church maintenance team for big events at the church. Ralph would go over Sal's measurements with him weekly. It really helped Sal to have someone acknowledge his effort and listen to his funny stories.

Sal was committed to the whole process. So when I mentioned consequences, he took that seriously. He said after about a minute's thought, "There's one thing I hate doing more than anything." I asked what that was, and he said, "Push-ups. My drill sergeant and a ranking officer would have me do them for any infraction."

As I said earlier, Sal was fifty-four years old. Sal was also quite large around the middle, so this wasn't going to be an easy consequence. He agreed he would drop and do ten push-ups for every swear word directed at an object and fifteen push-ups every time he used a swear word in front of another person.

Sal was definitely committed. He met with Ralph weekly and went over his object swearing, swearing around others, and his push-ups. Sal did his push-ups almost immediately. It took Sal forty-one days to stop swearing. It's been over six months, and Sal hasn't relapsed on this at all. He learned some other words from Ralph that he could say when projects didn't go exactly as planned, and he feels much better about himself. Sal figured out how getting a grip on things that are controlling you works, and he applied these principles to a few other rough spots that he had to get a grip on as well.

Sal's story is a great story of getting a grip on what is controlling you. Although I can tell you hundreds of great stories, no story will be more meaningful to you than your own sweet story of getting a grip on what is controlling you.

So let's start getting a grip on it. You previously listed several behaviors. By now you probably have at least one priority behavior to focus on. Now let's walk through your plan step-by-step. First, identify the behavior of which you want to get control.

Table 14-1: Road Map for Getting a Grip

My behavior is ______________________________

The issues I feel I need to be honest about are (use a separate sheet of paper if necessary):

1. ______________________________
2. ______________________________
3. ______________________________
4. ______________________________
5. ______________________________
6. ______________________________
7. ______________________________
8. ______________________________
9. ______________________________
10. ______________________________

I have officially made a decision to break this behavior.

- ☐ Yes, the ______day of ________________, 20________
- ☐ No

I have needed to do some cleansing the temple work.

- Yes, the _____ day of ______________, 20_______
- No

I have addressed the issues of forgiveness with

Myself on the date of ______________, 20_______

God on the date of ______________, 20_______

Others:

1. ______________________ on the date of ______________, 20_______
2. ______________________ on the date of ______________, 20_______
3. ______________________ on the date of ______________, 20_______
4. ______________________ on the date of ______________, 20_______
5. ______________________ on the date of ______________, 20_______
6. ______________________ on the date of ______________, 20_______
7. ______________________ on the date of ______________, 20_______
8. ______________________ on the date of ______________, 20_______
9. ______________________ on the date of ______________, 20_______
10. ______________________ on the date of ______________, 20_______

I have made a full disclosure to ________________________ on the date of ______________, 20_______

I have started to apply the five positive behaviors on:

1. Pray ______________, 20_______
2. Read ______________, 20_______
3. Meetings ________________, 20________

4. Calls ____________, 20______

5. Pray ____________, 20______

My specific behavioral goals are:

1. ____

____

2. ____

____

3. ____

____

My measurement for these goals is:

1. ____

____

2. ____

____

3. ____

The primary person who will hold me accountable as I get a grip on what has been controlling me is ______________________

We will meet______times a week for______weeks.

The negative consequences for my behaviors are:

1. ____

____

2. ____

____

3. ____

____

Use the chart on page 229 to track the first thirty days of your journey to get a grip on your behavior. Check off the tools you use each day and add them up for a daily score under the "Rate Yourself" column. This tracking exercise will help you stay on track with your goals. Note: I have provided three tracking records to allow you to work on three behaviors. Remember, this is the maximum amount of behaviors you should attempt to work on at one time.

You have just completed the road map for getting a grip on what has been controlling you. You can now get there! Once you have control over this area of your life, you will have learned a process that can lead to getting a grip on several other areas of your life also.

Imagine that you can possess a process that can keep control of any out-of-control behaviors that are trying to control you. You can intelligently look at yourself and say, "Attack," and actually win! I know I have personally applied these principles to my own out-of-control behavior and have freedom from some areas that have been controlling me for more than twenty years. I am definitely a work in progress but with a known process of maintaining control in my life.

My hope is that you will try the process to get a grip on your out-of-control behaviors. God wants us free so that we can best reflect Him and serve others. I know you may have questions throughout your process; our tendency is to avoid the painful or the difficult. This process requires that you go through both.

I have written many pages for you, and now it is your turn to write your story. It might start with becoming honest, then ridding yourself of anger, forgiving, finding someone to confide in, setting up good behaviors, measurement, accountability, and consequences. These steps are like the parts of a motor.

Once the pieces of the motor are in place, your story becomes like a luxury vehicle. You look great, feel great, and are moving through life with less resistance and more self-respect than before. You deserve the ride! After all, you paid for it with all you had to do to get here!

Now the wind is in your hair, the joy is back in your heart, and you have control over what has been controlling you. You're free and happy to be so. It's been great traveling with you, and I wish you the best as you cruise down this highway we call life!

God bless.

Table 14-2: My Tracking Record for Behavior: ____________________

	Pray	*Read*	*Meeting*	*Call*	*Measure*	*Accountability*	*Rate self*
Day 1							
Day 2							
Day 3							
Day 4							
Day 5							
Day 6							
Day 7							
Day 8							
Day 9							
Day 10							
Day 11							
Day 12							
Day 13							
Day 14							
Day 15							
Day 16							
Day 17							
Day 18							
Day 19							
Day 20							
Day 21							
Day 22							
Day 23							
Day 24							
Day 25							
Day 26							
Day 27							
Day 28							
Day 29							
Day 30							

Table 14-2: My Tracking Record for Behavior: ____________________

	Pray	*Read*	*Meeting*	*Call*	*Measure*	*Accountability*	*Rate self*
Day 1							
Day 2							
Day 3							
Day 4							
Day 5							
Day 6							
Day 7							
Day 8							
Day 9							
Day 10							
Day 11							
Day 12							
Day 13							
Day 14							
Day 15							
Day 16							
Day 17							
Day 18							
Day 19							
Day 20							
Day 21							
Day 22							
Day 23							
Day 24							
Day 25							
Day 26							
Day 27							
Day 28							
Day 29							
Day 30							

Table 14-2: My Tracking Record for Behavior: ____________

	Pray	*Read*	*Meeting*	*Call*	*Measure*	*Accountability*	*Rate self*
Day 1							
Day 2							
Day 3							
Day 4							
Day 5							
Day 6							
Day 7							
Day 8							
Day 9							
Day 10							
Day 11							
Day 12							
Day 13							
Day 14							
Day 15							
Day 16							
Day 17							
Day 18							
Day 19							
Day 20							
Day 21							
Day 22							
Day 23							
Day 24							
Day 25							
Day 26							
Day 27							
Day 28							
Day 29							
Day 30							

Dr. Douglas Weiss provides national and international conferences for issues facing couples, singles, men, and women. He also provides three-day intensives for individuals and couples every week in his Colorado Springs office.

Dr. Weiss also provides telephone counseling for anyone trying to get a grip on his or her life.

For more information, please contact Dr. Weiss at:

Web site: www.drdougweiss.com
E-mail: heart2heart@xc.org
Telephone: 719-278-3708